The
MARKET
PLANNING
GUIDE

SIXTH EDITION

CREATING A PLAN TO SUCCESSFULLY MARKET YOUR BUSINESS, PRODUCT, OR SERVICE

David H. Bangs, Jr.

Dearborn™
Trade Publishing
A **Kaplan Professional** Company

This publication is designed to provide accurate and authoritative information in regard to the subject matter covered. It is sold with the understanding that the publisher is not engaged in rendering legal, accounting, or other professional service. If legal advice or other expert assistance is required, the services of a competent professional person should be sought.

Vice President and Publisher: Cynthia A. Zigmund
Editorial Director: Donald J. Hull
Acquisitions Editor: Mary B. Good
Senior Managing Editor: Jack Kiburz
Cover Design: Design Solutions
Interior Design and Composition: Eliot House Productions

Published by Dearborn Trade Publishing, a Kaplan Professional Company

Printed in the United States of America

02 03 04 05 10 9 8 7 6 5 4 3 2 1

Library of Congress Cataloging-in-Publication Data

Bangs, David H.
   The market planning guide: creating a plan to successfully market your business, product, or service / David H. Bangs, Jr. —6th ed.
        p.   cm.
   Includes bibliographical references and index.
   ISBN 0-7931-5971-7 (pbk.)
   1. Marketing—Planning 2. Small business—Planning 3. New business enterprises—Planning. I. Title.
   HF5415.122.B36 2002
   658.8'02—dc21

                                                          2002007946

CONTENTS

INTRODUCTION

This book, the sixth edition of *The Market Planning Guide*, is my latest attempt to help you wrestle with the central problem facing your business: How can you attract enough customers willing and ready to buy your products and services at a price that yields you a profit? To make this more difficult, you have to answer that question in a highly competitive and rapidly changing world.

My favorite definition of marketing is the creation, satisfaction and retention of customers. Any business (more generally, any organization) will thrive only as long as it can come up with a steady stream of new customers. Even if you start with a steady base of loyal customers, roughly 30 percent of that base will erode each year due to fluctuations in the economy, people moving out of your trading area, the encroachment of new and indirect competitors, modification in tastes and habits, and a host of other changes. This is inevitable. Change happens.

Marketing is a challenge for all businesses, not just small ones. Look at two recent examples of marketing mismanagement. Kmart, caught between the low-cost provider Wal-Mart and the better positioning of Target, couldn't decide where to focus its efforts. The blue-light specials, which worked brilliantly in the '70s and '80s, lost out to Wal-Mart's "lower prices all the times" strategy and Target's more exciting and slightly more upscale offerings. Stock-out problems didn't help Kmart either; half-empty shelves have little appeal in a retail environment. Kmart did do a lot of things right—the linkage with Martha Stewart provided some ray of hope. But the major strategic blunder of lost customer focus did Kmart in. If you don't know who your customers are, how can you possibly know what they want that you can provide?

The other major blunder is Enron. My guess is that towards the end they had no idea what business they were in. Originally they traded energy, buying energy here and selling it over there. But what kind of business were they at the end of 2001? A trader of financial instruments called futures? A gambling casino, plunging heavily on derivatives? (Remember Orange County's bankruptcy a few years back? Long Term Capital's bailout? Derivatives are dangerous even for the most sophisticated traders!) What was Enron buying and selling—energy, water, or who knows what else? One of the major keys to marketing success is to know what business you are in and be able to communicate that knowledge to employers, customers, prospects, investors, and other stakeholders clearly and succinctly. And that means knowing what you sell, to what market, and in what fashion.

If you are in a small business you have less margin for error than the Enrons and Kmarts. You don't have the capital to keep going if you make a serious error in your marketing. If you are in a larger business where your career depends on meeting marketing goals that you may or may not have had a hand in setting, the business will most likely keep chugging along without you. Whether you run a small business unit or something larger, it is in your interest to do what you can to correctly market your products. In any business, some internal marketing will be necessary. You have to sell an idea to your staff, boss, and colleagues. You can't escape the marketing imperative.

This book is structured around 30 questions. As you proceed, new ideas crop up, new doors open, and old doors shut. You'll find that you will revise, revisit, amplify, reject, and otherwise improve your plan over time. This is an organic process, not a neat linear job where you can check off Question 1, Question 2, and so on. Think of concocting a stew—you need a few ingredients, some tools, and time to let the flavors blend. You also want to make subtle changes (add paprika, garlic, grated some cheese). Presentation is important: What does the final result look like? Your marketing plan evolves in the same way. You need a few ingredients. You don't add everything you can find. Selectivity is important. You need information. You need time to mull things over. You need to be flexible enough to make the small changes that separate a good marketing plan from a bland, dull, useless plan. And of course in making both stews and marketing plans, experience will ensure better, more consistent results.

My friend, Pete Worrell, sent me a quotation from Roger Babson, the financier and philanthropist who called the 1929 stock market crash:

> Experience has taught me that there is one chief reason why some people succeed and others fail. The difference is not one of knowing, but of doing. The successful man is not so superior in ability as in action. So far as success can be reduced to a formula, it consists of this: doing what you know you should do.

In *The Market Planning Guide* I try to help you know what you should do. I wish you success!

—Andy Bangs
<andybangs@attbi.com>

CHAPTER ONE

THE QUICK STRATEGIC MARKETING PLAN

The best place to start a marketing plan is at the beginning, with an understanding of what you hope to accomplish in your business and a feel for the strategies that will best help you to achieve those goals.

The rationale for all of the effort in this chapter is that if you do the right things, then you can worry about doing things right—but if you do the wrong things, it doesn't much matter how well you do them. You could be the best marketer or manager in the world, but if you aim for the wrong market, or have the wrong products you will still go broke. Being in the wrong industry at the wrong time or in the most promising industry with the wrong resources guarantees that you won't succeed. The list goes on and on. The point is simple: pick your focus, where you concentrate your efforts, very carefully. Specialize if you can, but in any event strive to identify strengths to build on and opportunities to grasp, all the while making sure to improve weak areas and avoid those problematic threats you cannot control.

Every business is run according to some strategy, a guiding set of goals and assumptions that result in a directed approach to a business opportunity or situation. "Trusting to luck" is a strategy. "Reacting to outside pressure" is another. "Inertia" and "habit" and "business as usual" are also strategies, though not particularly good ones. The question isn't whether or not your business will pursue a strategy but whether the strategy you select will be the most useful for your business at this time, given your resources, interests, markets, and competition. A strategic plan based on analysis of your strengths, weaknesses, opportunities, and threats (these will be explained later) will help you identify and then accomplish your business goals.

Every business is run according to some strategy, a guiding set of goals and assumptions that result in a directed approach to a business opportunity or situation.

Strategic marketing, which is simply marketing that has been planned to take advantage of your strengths and minimize your weaknesses, starts with a single question:

QUESTION 1

What business are you in?

This is not easy to answer.

There are lots of ways you could answer this question. A *product definition* lists the products or services you offer. A *technology definition* stresses your technological competencies. A *market definition* defines your business in terms of your current and prospective customers. A *conceptual definition*[1] gives a sense of what your business is all about, and what it hopes to become and how.

To adequately describe your business, answer the following questions. Don't aim for 100 percent accuracy. You can fine-tune your definition later.

If you have a business plan you will have already gone through these exercises. If not, ask yourself and your colleagues these five questions:

1. *What are our products and services?* Your business definition is based on what you sell.
2. *Who are our customers?* Your present customer base and the target markets you choose to serve help focus the definition further.
3. *What would our customers and prospects like to buy from us?* Your products and services must match your customers' desires, not yours.
4. *Why do our customers buy from us?* There are plenty of competitors for every business, and a wide range of products and services for your customers and prospects to choose from.
5. *What sets our business apart from our competitors?* What is distinctive or unusual about your business? If you can differentiate yourself from your competitors in the eyes of your markets you seize a strong advantage.

These five core questions are more difficult to answer than you may expect. If you are inexperienced, take advantage of the Small Business Administration's (SBAs) Service Corps of Retired Executives (SCORE) and Small Business Development Center (SBDC) programs. These are free, paid by your tax dollar, and effective resources. Visit the SBAs Web site at <www.sba.gov> for more information. You should also have your employees, advisers, and other stakeholders help you rough out the answers to these questions. Their input will enrich your decisions.

Your definition of your business determines the direction your business takes. If you can state clearly and succinctly what you sell, to whom,

If you are inexperienced, take advantage of the Small Business Administration's (SBAs) Service Corps of Retired Executives (SCORE) and Small Business Development Center (SBDC) programs.

---

[1] Sometimes called an airplane definition: If you tried to explain your business to someone as you circled O'Hare for yet another 20 minutes, what would you say?

and why they buy from you and not from someone else you are well on the way to creating an effective marketing plan.

There is no "right" definition. A series of answers will evolve as your business changes. Your products, services, and markets change all the time. So does your competitive position. Other people will copy what you do well and compete for your customers on price, quality, service or wherever you appear vulnerable.

Figure 1.1: The Business Definition Worksheet will help you capture the important parts of your business. Don't aim for elaborate answers or

---

1. Name and date the business was established: Montville, CPA

2. Check one: The business is a:
    ❏ corporation   ❏ Sub S or a Limited type corporation   ☒ partnership   ❏ sole proprietorship

3. Check one: Our customers are primarily:
    ❏ individuals   ❏ corporate   ❏ institutional   ☒ other (*describe briefly*) small business owners

4. Current products and services include   tax prep., management, advisory services

5. My five closest competitors are
    1. Bridge & Silverman
    2. SB & R
    3. Purdy, Bernstein
    4. General Business Services
    5.

6. Possible competition could come from:
    a. other companies:
    b. technologies: tax software, expert systems
    c. industries:

7. Allies actual or prospective include: _____

    _____

8. Is demand for my products or services increasing or decreasing?:   increasing

9. Products or services I might discontinue are   personal tax returns (not business)

10. Products or services I might introduce are   speciality in industry segments

11. Markets I might exit are   doesn't apply

12. Markets I might enter are   specific business segment: auto and equipment dealers?

13. My company is unique because   don't know—better look into this

14. Right now my company's biggest marketing obstacle is   lack of time

15. Our biggest marketing opportunity is   specializing in small business markets

16. Our overall business goals and growth plans are   sales of $500K in 3 years; add another CPA?

FIGURE 1.1 The Business Definition Worksheet

profound statements in it. Just hit the high spots. You'll have plenty of chances to return to your business definition later.

The next step in creating a quick strategic plan is to write a mission statement, a condensed version of your business definition.

Mission statements do not bind your hands. They liberate you from continually grappling with strategic decisions. Frances Hesselbein, former head of the Girl Scouts of America, put the reason for working out a mission statement brilliantly:

> We kept asking ourselves very simple questions. What is our business? Who is our customer? And what does the customer consider value? We really are here for one reason: to help a girl reach her highest potential... *More than any one thing, that made the difference. Because when you are clear about your mission, corporate goals and operating objectives flow from it.*
>
> ("Profiting from the Nonprofits," *Business Week*, March 26, 1990. Italics added.)

In other words, the effort you put into these basic strategic questions save you effort in the long run.

Mission statements may seem to be a waste of time, but they serve a vital purpose: they let everyone know what the organization is striving to achieve. To prove the need for mission statements in your business, ask some of your colleagues (at least five, which might include customers,

> The next step in creating a quick strategic plan is to write a mission statement, a condensed version of your business definition.

PICKING AN INITIAL STRATEGY

John Case, writing in the *Boston Globe* (August 10, 1994) proposed a simple way to pick an initial strategy. Are you in a commodity, specialty, or head-to-head business?

- If you are in a commodity business, one where there is little or no perceived difference between your product or service and that offered by competitors, the suggested strategy is to be the low-cost producer or supplier. Competition will be driven by price. Agricultural products exemplify commodity businesses.

- Specialty businesses, such as specialty retailers or ethnic restaurants, compete by carving out a niche in the marketplace and raising barriers to entry into that niche. For example, if you run a bicycle shop, you might try to become the local authority on mountain bicycles and gear, sponsor races, put on training and informational workshops, and make sure to stock the newest and best equipment. This would make it very difficult for anyone else to dislodge you from your niche. Note that you would not compete on price.

- Most small businesses are what Case calls "head-to-head" businesses. These should find a niche and fill it; that is, adopt a strategy of finding out what would be especially attractive to their markets about their products, services or delivery systems and then providing it. Establishing what Rosser Reeves called a "unique selling proposition," a competitive advantage that can be maintained and built on over time, pays off handsomely. Think of Frank Perdue and the humble chicken.

board members, staff, or other stakeholders) to write a single sentence describing what the business is about. You'll get widely different answers. "And if people close to the business are this confused, what are your customers thinking?"

Why do mission statements have such a poor reputation? Too many of them are drivel, simplistic God, Mom, and apple pie statements that blather meaninglessly about excellence, quality, delighting the customer, upholding basic American values, and so forth. Good mission statements take time and effort. They don't just happen.

The following are all effective mission statements:

American Red Cross. The American Red Cross is a humanitarian organization, led by volunteers, that provides relief to victims of disasters and helps people prevent, prepare for, and respond to emergencies. It does this through services that are consistent with its Congressional Charter and the principles of the International Red Cross Movement.

Use your completed Business Description Worksheet as your guide. Circle or otherwise highlight key phrases in Figure 1.1. Jot them down where you think they belong in the following categories. Write down the single most important goal for your business. Then condense the result into one or two short sentences. This will result in a mission statement that accurately reflects your business's purposes.

Customers: _small business owners_

Products or services: _tax & MAS or consulting_

Markets: _local (within 10–15 mile radius)_

Economic objectives: _make money, profit, stable revenue base_

Beliefs, values, and aspirations: _independence, concern for community, want to make a difference, make a good living_

Distinctive competence: What are we *really* good at?: _helping small business owners max revenues, hold down costs, use info._

Concern for employees: _provide reasonable compensation and benefits, provide freedom to do their jobs with minimum supervision_

Mission Statement

Provide tax and management advisory services to local small business owners, helping them to grow, and providing our employees with a rewarding working environment.

FIGURE 1.2 Mission Statement Worksheet

Wal-Mart. To give ordinary folks the chance to buy the same thing as rich people.

Disney. To make people happy.

Domino's Pizza. To be the leader in off-premises pizza convenience.

McDonald's. To be the world's best quick service restaurant experience. Being the best means providing outstanding quality, service, cleanliness, and value, so that we make every customer in every restaurant smile.

These all pass the 45-second test so beloved of venture capitalists. They let everyone know what the business is all about—and do so without meaningless boasting bombast.

The business definition and mission statement make it much simpler to select and evaluate appropriate long-term goals for your business. By taking a long time frame (three to five years) as the span of your quick strategic plan, you make it easier to keep your business focused on the goals you choose to pursue.

The next step is to conduct a SWOT Analysis of your company. "SWOT" stands for "Strengths, Weaknesses, Opportunities, and Threats." This is fairly straightforward for most small businesses. A word of advice: the more of your employees you involve in the SWOT analysis the better.

SCOPING OUT THE EXTERNAL ENVIRONMENT: THE PEST ANALYSIS

Your business operates in many environments, ordinarily divided into the internal environment (within the organization, hence somewhat under your control) and the external environment (outside the organization, hence only marginally or not under your control). A PEST analysis looks at those factors you have no control over:

- *Political issues.* What political factors might affect your marketing plans? Think of the regulations you have to meet, pending legislation, tax issues.

- *Economic factors.* What's going on in the economy at large? Where are interest rates heading? Inflation? The stock market? Disposable income?

- *Sociocultural factors.* We have an increasingly diverse population. What are the implications for your business of the surge in Spanish speaking people (for example), with their religious, cultural, and social customs?

- *Technological factors.* Technological change cannot be ignored. What will affect your business? Look at how Amazon.com revolutionized the book market by using computers to continuously communicate with customers and keep them aware of new books, tapes, DVDs, and by sending e-mail alerts.

Garner materials for an ongoing PEST analysis as a routine activity. You'll find plenty of material in newspapers, magazines and trade association publications and through daily contacts. Timely information is more valuable than stale information—and it provides a competitive advantage.

SWOT ANALYSIS

SWOT analysis is a blunt tool. Because it is subjective, based on people's perceptions rather than hard data, take the results with a grain of salt. The systematic examination of SWOT will provide lots of ideas and insights that you will have to prioritize. That's your job.

Internal environment	Strengths	Weaknesses
External environment	Opportunities	Threats
	Build on these	Mitigate these

Successful business owners find that a periodic meeting with all employees to work through the following five forms not only gives rise to some extraordinarily insightful comments, it also makes sure that the employees buy in to the planning process. It can take as little as half a day to set the broad directions.

SWOT begins by looking at internal strengths and weaknesses. Since the important areas vary from one business to the next, customize these forms to reflect your particular business. The first eight areas are common to all businesses, and should always be examined.

Use of Figure 1.3: Internal Analysis: Strengths and Weaknesses is easy. For each key area, ask whether it is a strength or a weakness. It may be both—people sometimes have different views. What you are looking for is a rough profile of your business's internal performance. You want to be able to capitalize on the strengths and defend or improve weaknesses.

Now look to the external environments where your business operates. While these factors are not under your control, if you examine how they will affect you, you can take precautionary or preemptive action. Again, this is fairly simple. For each factor ask what opportunities and threats to the success of your business are coming up. Technological factors include new or improved technologies. Think of what happened to the typesetting industry when desktop publishing became affordable. Regulatory and legal factors are in constant flux. You might grow into a new area of legal exposure; for example if you employ 15 people you have to comply with the Americans with Disabilities Act. The economic environments—local, national and international—have obvious impact on your ability to reach financial goals. Be aware of them.

You want to be able to capitalize on the strengths and defend or improve weaknesses.

Factor	Strengths	Weaknesses
1. Profitability		needs improvement
2. Sales and marketing		x
3. Quality	x	
4. Customer service	x	
5. Productivity	N/A	
6. Financial resources		x—need more capital?
7. Financial management		
8. Operations	—questionable—(look into this)	
9. Production and distribution	N/A	
10. Personnel development	x	
* Reputation	very good with small business owners	

FIGURE 1.3 Internal Analysis: Strengths and Weaknesses

Figure 1.4 is not intended to be exhaustive—it is meant to be suggestive. If you face different external factors, add them.

This is not brain surgery. Don't dwell too long on these forms (Figures 1.3 and 1.4.) You are looking for major forces that will impact your business, not for some super subtle wrinkle. Strategizing has to be broad brush. The details, the goals and objectives and implementation of the strategies are another matter.

Now go back over the completed Figures 1.3 and 1.4. Pick no more than five strengths and opportunities to work on, and no more than five weaknesses and threats to worry about. Pick them carefully. You limit the

Factor	Opportunities	Threats
Current customers	upgrade them—MAS, etc.	
Prospect	lots of small businesses currently underserved	expensive to gain new clients
Competition		strong and well-managed crowded field, big companies now trying to enter the market
Technology	develop programs (very specialized); increase productivity; "bells and whistles" for better demos; teach people how to use tax programs	
Political climate		
Government and other regulatory bodies	always new taxes and regulations!	
Legal		
Economic environment	recovering	

FIGURE 1.4 External Analysis: Opportunities and Threats

The most important strengths we possess and the best opportunities we face are:

1. _(o) underserved small business market—that's growing_

2. _(s) reputation for quality with current base_

3. _(o) focus on small business owners ONLY_

4. _____

5. _____

The most dangerous weaknesses and threats we face are:

1. _(w) capital: underfinanced_

2. _(t) new competitors_

3. _____

4. _____

5. _____

FIGURE 1.5 SWOT Summary

> **T**he most
> important decision
> is what to
> focus on.

choice to make sure that you focus attention on areas with the greatest payback. If you only pick one or two strengths and opportunities, or weaknesses and threats, fine. If they are really important, this choice will drive your marketing plans[2].

Use the next two forms, Figure 1.6: Building on Strengths and Opportunities, and Figure 1.7: Shore Up Weaknesses, Avoid Threats to quickly establish a strategic plan, the goal of this introductory chapter. Figure 1.5: SWOT Summary sets these up. The essence of small business strategy is to find and dominate small market niches, please customers better than the next business, and keep it all simple so the strategies can be communicated effectively. The *actions* you come up with become your strategies.

By now you have made important strategic decisions and set your priorities. The most important decision is what to focus on. The next two (and final) steps in creating a quick strategic plan turn the ideas you have developed into long-term goals (three to five years out) and then turn the goals into specific short-term objectives. Your goals and objectives are the foundation of your marketing plan.

Return to Figures 1.6 and 1.7. Goals are the desired result of the actions you choose to do. Goals have to be *measurable* (most often in dollars or

---

[2] Other plans that will be affected include your annual business plan, any financing plans, and (if appropriate for your business) your operating plans.

FOUR KEY STRATEGIES

Four strategies for small business owners to follow include the following:

1. *Focus.* Small businesses do not have resources to squander, so it is vital that they concentrate their efforts where they can achieve their most important goals. This is hard to do—it takes a great deal of discipline to pass up apparent (as opposed to real and related) opportunities and stick with what you are best at doing.

2. *Personalize.* This is the greatest strength that small businesses possess. You can infuse your business with your personality. If you focus your efforts on a target market and know your customers well, you can offer a climate that no big company can match. The "feel" or personality of a small business is an important asset.

3. *Specialize or Customize.* Small businesses work best in niche markets. This is another aspect of focus: offer products and services that your markets demand. Specialization is one way to do this. A store specializing in kitchen gadgets will do better than one that offers a bit of everything including kitchen gadgets. Customizing takes specializing even further—also a form of focusing on the customers' needs.

4. *Simplify.* Keep strategies simple in order to communicate with your markets and employees. A complex strategy not only blurs your focus, it also confuses everyone who encounters it.

To build on our major strengths and opportunities listed on Figure 1.5, we will take the following actions:

#1 Strength or opportunity	underserved market that's growing
Action	set up system to seek out and approach those businesses before anyone else
#2 Strength or opportunity	our excellent reputation
Action	leverage word of mouth, ask for referrals and endorsements
#3 Strength or opportunity	focus on small business
Action	promotions, identify ALL businesses fitting our criteria, create identity as small business specialists

FIGURE 1.6 Building on Strengths and Opportunities

To shore up the weaknesses and avoid the threats listed on Figure 1.5, we will take the following actions:

#1 Weakness or threat	lack of capital
Action	invest more!—-and invest profits

#2 Weakness or threat	new competitors
Action	more personal service, faster response, stress local nature of this practice, continuity (same person year after year)

#3 Weakness or threat

Action

FIGURE 1.7 Shore Up Weaknesses, Avoid Threats

STRATEGIC GOALS

Qualitative goals are defined in the strategic planning process.

Positioning

What is the position of your business in its markets and among its competitors? How is it perceived by your target markets?

Segmentation

What segments of the market do you want to attract?

Culture

What is the culture of your business?

Differentiation

How does your business differ from its competitors? What are the special skills and competencies of your business?

Social responsibilities

What purposes does your business serve beyond its own survival and profitability?

GOALS AND OBJECTIVES

The distinction between GOALS and OBJECTIVES is not just semantic. Goals are long-range, anywhere from a year to many years out, and help you maintain strategic direction. Objectives are short-range, specific activities that are tactics to move you towards your long-term goals. Their areas will overlap—market share, profitability, growth, or product development goals will spill over into their correlative objectives. It is a close relationship.

Both goals and objectives should be SMART:

Specific. Use specific terms. Exactly what do you want to achieve?

Measurable. Objectives must be quantified.

Attainable. If the objectives are not attainable, why bother?

Realistic. They should be attainable with the resources you have available.

Timed. Start and end dates (especially end dates) make the objectives more real.

Goal:	sales to $500,000 in 3 yrs.; $100,000 profit
Person responsible:	RM & GL
Due date:	3 yrs. out
Goal:	earn $80K/yr.
Person responsible:	RM
Due date:	next year
Goal:	semi-retire in 5 yrs.
Person responsible:	RM
Due date:	5 yrs.
Goal:	develop services packages (financial management and consulting, less accounting)
Person responsible:	GL
Due date:	6–12 months

FIGURE 1.8 Long-Term Goals

units), have a *deadline*, and be someone's *responsibility*. Goals also have to be believable and achievable. If the people responsible don't believe the goals are worthwhile, they won't make the effort necessary to achieve the goal. If the goals aren't achievable (given the resources available and conditions that apply), then those responsible for achieving the goals will be frustrated no matter how hard they try and eventually your goals will be ignored.

Goals direct and control actions. They give you something to aim at, some way to measure progress and answer the question, "How am I doing?" The clearer you can make your goals the better; clear goals make communicating strategy a lot easier than vague, fuzzy goal-like aims such as "make more money" or "increase profits."

Take your time with this step. Choose your goals carefully. You might achieve them. How would meeting these goals impact your finances, your personnel, your plant and equipment? What would it do to your life outside the business (time commitments especially)? Although these aren't part of the marketing plan, they can affect it.

> The clearer you can make your goals the better.

In order to achieve the goals set in Figure 1.8, break them down into short-term objectives to be accomplished within the next year:

Long-term goal #1:	sales to $325,000 this year
Short-term objectives:	focus on identified small businesses (both clients and prospects); more vigorous promotion
Long-term goal #2:	RM salary and retirement
Short-term objectives:	personal financial plan
Long-term goal #3:	develop services package
Short-term objectives:	survey clients, check with AICPA, use competitor files, connect with local Small Business Development Center

FIGURE 1.9 Turning Goals into Objectives

Once the goals have been selected and approved, the next step is to turn them into short-term objectives (see Figure 1.9). *For the purposes of a marketing plan, treat the objectives as goals: assign responsibility, measurements, and due dates.*

This concludes the quick strategic plan. Based on the primary strategy to "build on strengths, shore up weaknesses," your goals and objectives make sense for your business, at this time, given your resources and capabilities. This is where your marketing plan begins.

Summary for Chapter One

- You answered the key strategic question: What business are you in?
- You wrote a mission statement.
- You performed a SWOT analysis to determine what your business's strengths and weaknesses are, and what opportunities and threats it will face over the next three to five years.
- You chose a general strategy based on the SWOT analysis, turned the strategy into a coherent set of goals, and turned the goals into a preliminary set of objectives to be accomplished over the next year.

CHAPTER TWO

MARKETING OVERVIEW

"Marketing" is the complex process of creating customers for your products and services. A marketing plan is a written document that helps you manage this process—including the action steps needed to make the plan work.

Your marketing plan requires answers to 30 major questions. These questions are labeled Question 1, Question 2, and so forth. A complete list of these questions is provided in Appendix One.

Writing the plan is easy. You don't write the plan itself until you've done 95 percent of the work. The tough part of market planning is a careful examination of your business, including

- product and service analysis;
- analysis of your markets and your position in that market;
- analysis of the strengths and weaknesses of your business.

Planning cannot be done in a vacuum. The first step is to take a broad overview of your marketing efforts, including current markets, products, and services, in the context of current economic and competitive conditions. You did this in Chapter One when you answered Question 1: What business am I in?

> You don't write the plan itself until you've done 95 percent of the work.

QUESTION 2

What do you sell?

What are you selling: Computers? Landscape designs? Real estate? Clothing? Legal advice? Fish? Medical services? Baseball bats?

CUSTOMER FOCUS

Customer focus forces your business to succeed.

There are two ways to view customer focus. First, adopt your customers' (actual or prospective) focus on your products and services. Second, all your efforts will be based on meeting your customers' needs.

If you target your market effectively, you will have a manageable number of customers who you can learn a great deal about—how they think, why they buy, when they buy, what their preferences might be. You will be able to learn what benefits they seek so you can choose to address those demands. Knowing the benefits they seek allows you to market your goods and services economically and effectively, using messages and media that they will see and be influenced by.

In a wider sense, customer focus helps you make strategically helpful decisions in all aspects of your business. As examples, you would choose what to offer in light of your market's desires. You would choose a location or means of distribution primarily because it is convenient for your customers, and only secondarily convenient for you. You would hire, train, and manage staff to better serve your customers and prospects—and your staff would serve the customers the way the customers want to be served.

You cannot do this unless you focus on your best customers and prospects. Ask them what they want. They'll tell you.

In Chapter Three you will return to your product/service list from a different angle. For now, just list the products and/or services you sell in Figure 2.2. You will fill in the "target market" column later.

QUESTION 3

Who are your target markets?

Target marketing is a simple concept. You have a limited number of marketing dollars, so you want to invest them wisely. Your business has a potential market consisting of a vaguely defined group of people who might buy your products. In order to invest your money wisely you have to narrow that broad group down to those persons (or persons in particular institutions) most likely to buy from you.

Many potential buyers are too far away geographically, can't afford your prices, don't want to change suppliers, prefer to deal locally, or are unlikely for other reasons to become your customers. Recognizing these limitations on your market is the first step towards target marketing. Next, identify the segments of the overall market which are most likely to buy from you. (See Chapter Four for more on this.)

What is target marketing? Look at Figure 2.1. The bull's-eye is worth $10 in sales, the first ring $5, the next ring $3, the final ring $1. Missing the target is a dead loss.

Now suppose you need $100 in sales to break even, and a marketing budget of $15 (for the sake of the illustration, think of that as 15 arrows).

In order to meet your $100 goal, you have to have a lot of bull's-eyes and very few misses. You need at least five bull's-eyes. Any fewer and you can't achieve your goal of $100. Needless to say, you'd take considerable care with each arrow.

To push the metaphor a bit further, you'd find that your marksmanship improves with practice, that taking careful note of surrounding conditions is important, and that focusing on your target pays off. Shooting at one random target after another is confusing, and makes your expensively gathered experience useless. So does changing your bow, or forgetting to keep score.

In marketing, you have to keep track of what you're up to. Fashions change. The economic climate changes. Products and services gain and lose value. Markets shift. But you will always have a finite number of arrows (marketing dollars), and you will always find that once you have the range on a target it pays off to keep shooting at that target until you have good reasons to shoot at a new one.

Target marketing is an ongoing five step process.

1. Who is most likely to buy from you? These people are at the center of your target market.
2. What characteristics (wants, needs, habits) do your best customers and prospects share? This information is used to segment or differentiate the market.
3. How big are the segments?
4. Rank the segments in terms of potential profitability for your business. You may need help here.

> In marketing, you have to keep track of what you're up to.

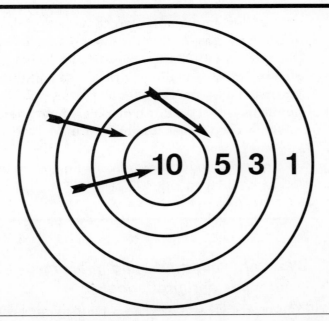

FIGURE 2.1 Target Marketing

If you have many products or services, try to bundle them together into no more than ten categories. You can always expand the list later—but for now, keep it simple.

	Product/Service	Target Markets
1.	business consulting	
2.	monthly accounting services	
3.	audits	
4.	tax return preparation	service and retail
5.	tax consultation	businesses
6.	tax representation	$700K to $5M
7.	special projects	in annual sales
8.	other accounting services	
9.		
10.		

FIGURE 2.2 Product/Service and Market List

5. What is the most profitable segment mix (in terms of ease and cost of sale, sales volume, and price)?

Just how important is target marketing? Kmart tried to serve a muddle of markets: cost-conscious shoppers, some more fashionable segments (their deals with Martha Stewart and Jaclyn Smith), and parents (Sesame Street). This was perilously close to an all-things-for-all-people approach. The result was confusion for all parties concerned. One reason for Kmart's problems is that a diffuse market is much harder to appeal to than a narrowly focused target. Target your market, focus your efforts on that market, and prosper.

For each product or service, who do you think the target markets are? Jot them down on Figure 2.2.

QUESTION 4

What are your marketing goals for next year? Your sales and profit goals?

You need two sets of goals: one for your business and one for yourself. Your personal goals come first. You want to be sure you don't commit your business to a strategy that runs counter to your personal wishes. Do you want to sell your business in a few years and retire? Build the business to Fortune 1000 size, or keep it small? Be a technological trailblazer? All of these have been cited by small-business owners, and each has profound marketing implications. These goals will be reached by attaining a series of short-term objectives (see Chapter One, Figure 1.9).

Some plausible marketing goals are increased dollar or unit sales, improved market share, greater profits, entry into new markets, abandoning a current market, and adopting a new technology or product line. Maybe you want to improve your company's image, advertising, or promotional efforts. Or implement a new pricing strategy or distribution process.

Be general. You will reexamine and refocus your goals. To turn these vague goals into objectives, you have to do more. Objectives involve specific numbers and time frames. For now, just jot down the broad marketing goals you would like to achieve over the next year and over the next three years. While your marketing plan will cover only one year in detail, longer-range goals provide directional stability and help you maintain your focus.

Sales and profit goals should be precise.

If you have a small number of product or service lines, break the goals down further. But even an aggregate number is helpful; you can break it down later. For each product or service and target market of Figure 2.2, forecast sales for the next year in Figure 2.4. A worst case/best case/most likely case approach makes this somewhat easier and more accurate than just guessing. A product by product approach produces a more accurate forecast than lumping all your sales together in one undifferentiated heap.

> A product by product approach produces a more accurate forecast than lumping all your sales together in one undifferentiated heap.

---

1. How much money do you want, or need, to earn?

   $80,000 salary, plus partnership profit

2. What sort of lifestyle is desirable for you and your family?

   affluent

3. How big do you want your business to become?

   gross revenues to $500,000/yr. in 3 yrs.

4. How will your business reflect you and your values?

   be fair to employees and clients

5. How much risk do you want to take? In what areas?

   not a business with risks, want achievable goals

6. What do you want to achieve over the next five years?

   semi-retire in 5 years

FIGURE 2.3 Personal Goals for the Business

Product	Worst Case	Most Likely Case	Best Case
1. consulting	$50	$85	$100
2. monthly	30	45	45
3. audits	15	20	25
4. tax prep.	30	45	50
5. tax consulting	30	45	55
6. special projects (industry-specific)	25	60	75
7. other	15	20	20
	$195	$320	$370

FIGURE 2.4 Best Case/Worst Case Approach

SALES FORECASTING BY WEIGHTED AVERAGE OR BAYESIAN ANALYSIS

Sales projections give most business owners fits, because the future seems so uncertain and projections seem so imprecise. There's merit to this concern—many of us share it. But there are various clues. Suppose you run a restaurant. Go to <www.restaurant.org/research/forecast_sales.cfm> to see the numbers put together by the National Restaurant Association to help its members look into the future. Most trade associations have similar information assembled by experts that can (when modified to your particular circumstances) give you direction.

Or go to <www.chanimal.com/html/projections.html> for a short list of projection techniques. Their example of Baseline Goal Setting is worth reading.

If you have a statistician available, look into techniques such as moving averages or the more recondite regression analyses. Computers have made their application fairly simple—though in 30 plus years working with small business owners I have yet to meet one who uses these techniques. Any finance textbook will show you how to use them.

Bayesian analysis is a technique based on giving carefully thought-out weights to various scenarios. For example, suppose you think you have a 60 percent chance of sales of $1,000,000 next year, a 10 percent chance of sales reaching $1,200,000, and a 20 percent chance of only hitting $950,000. A Bayesian Analysis would go like this:

Scenario	Sales	Percent	Forecast
	$1,000,000	70%	$700,000
	$1,200,000	10%	$120,000
	$950,000	20%	$190,000

The Bayesian analysis would yield a forecast of $1,010,000 (the sum of the three forecast numbers). The accuracy of such a forecast depends to a high degree on the weights and the probabilities—but then, all forecasts are "best guesstimates" anyway.

You may prefer to break down forecasts by salesperson or department. This chart is from <www.nafem.org/resources/pod/forms/form08.doc>.

Monthly Sales Projections

Salesperson or Department _____ Date _____

	New Business			Reorders			Total		
	Goal	Actual	Var.	Goal	Actual	Var.	Goal	Actual	Var.
January									
February									
March									
April									
May									
June									
July									
August									
September									
October									
November									
December									
Year									

Choose the technique you like best. No one technique is perfect, nor does any one method suit everyone.

For each product or product line, estimate what sales would be if everything goes wrong next year. Then estimate what sales would be if everything goes perfectly. Since neither case is likely, an in-between sales figure will be a more accurate forecast. This number (the "most likely case") is not an average of worst and best cases, but rather your considered opinion of what will happen to each product or service line over the next year.

Don't be surprised if filling out Figure 2.4 gets you to rethink and revise Figure 2.2. It should. Part of the value of the market plan is the process of continually rethinking how your product/services and target markets intersect.

Profit goals are harder to establish. If you know what profit you traditionally make as a percentage of sales, use the sales forecast and add a bit.

Marketing Goals

1. _develop program for small business financial management._
2. _develop more management accounting; shift from traditional accounting_
3. _marketing database of small businesses—$700K—$5M_
4. _work on identity definition_

Sales Goals for each Product/Service (see Figure 2.4 for next year's most likely figures)

		For next year	In three years
1.	_consulting_	$85	$125
2.	_monthly_	$45	$60
3.	_audits_	$20	$50
4.	_tax returns_	$45	$65
5.	_tax consultation_	$45	$90
6.	_special projects_	$60	$90
7.	_other_	$20	$20
	Sales Goals	$320	$500
	Profit Goals: 15% of sales	48	75

Comments:

_____

_____

_____

FIGURE 2.5 Preliminary Marketing, Sales, and Profit Goals

You don't want to set objectives too low, and you will (you hope) become more profitable with more sales. Experience will correct or corroborate your hopes.

Note that Figure 2.5 gives you both a dollar figure and a time frame. This makes your objectives more precise, which helps you set up benchmarks to test progress and measure improvement.

QUESTION 5

What might keep you from achieving these goals?

Possible barriers include cash flow or capital shortages, personnel deficiencies or inefficiencies, weak technology, stale product lines, pricing woes, declining or flat sales, strong new competitors, quality control problems, and many more.

Every company has limitations. A smart owner or manager knows what the problems are and addresses them. The ostrich-like manager, on the other hand, is always receiving nasty blind-side surprises. The SWOT analysis in Chapter One provides insight here. Look back at Figure 1.7:

Today's date _____

What problems am I avoiding?

1. _collections—get tougher with slow pays_ _____

2. _investing in promotion and marketing_ _____

3. _____

What problems might prevent us from reaching our marketing, sales, and profit goals?

1. _time—too few doing too much_ _____

2. _understaffed_ _____

3. _aggressive competitors_ _____ _add person in 6 months_ ___

4. _____

5. _____

What are we going to do about these problems? (See Figures 1.6 and 1.7.)

1. Assign responsibility to individuals to achieve solutions.   ×

2. Allocate resources and authority to these people.   ×

3. Establish benchmarks and deadlines to help them monitor their progress.   ×

FIGURE 2.6 Problems

Shore Up Weaknesses, Avoid Threats for the most important limitations your business faces.

Some problems are long term: A job shop printer has to be concerned about laser printing and desk top publishing, not because the technology is widespread but because it will be, and it will change his or her business climate. Being a supplier to a declining industry is a long-term problem. So is being located in a stagnant or declining local economy.

Product and service limitations might involve quality control, rejected raw inventories, stock-outs, delivery problems, lack of skilled service personnel, and old equipment that puts you at a time and cost disadvantage.

Know your limitations. Then correct them—or adjust your marketing plans to accommodate them. Follow Figure 2.6 and keep a list of problems that you think might get between you and your goals. The finest memory is not so firm as faded ink. Write them down.

Note that Figure 2.6 calls for action. A marketing plan has to be implemented, or it's a waste of time. Dramatic changes in your business will come from correcting errors and problems. More lasting and profitable, if less splashy, changes result from implementing a carefully thought-out marketing strategy.

Know your limitations. Then correct them—or adjust your marketing plans to accommodate them.

What is your marketing budget?

This is a trick question. If you have a marketing budget, you can answer it. If you don't, you have the most common problem: no budget at all. The second most common budgeting problem is relying on a reactive, sloppy, "whatever is available if I have no better use for it" excuse for a budget.

Marketing is as much a cost of doing business as rent or payroll. It isn't a "cost center" to cut at the first sign of slumping sales or reduce to boost profits for a month or two. If you don't have a marketing budget or if you think your current budget needs improvement, go no further. You must have a budget—unless you want to waste money and forego sales and profit improvement.

Another common method of setting a marketing budget is to allocate a fixed percentage of forecast sales on a calendar basis. You can get trade figures. Ask your business counselor, accountant, banker, or other financial experts such as editors of trade magazines. Ask other successful business owners. These trade averages will provide some useful guidelines.

Just remember that more than advertising and public relations come out of your marketing budget. What do sales cost you? Sales training? Preparation of window displays? Sales support and presentation pieces? Check out Figure 2.7 below. Your marketing budget has to reflect your business, not someone else's.

Look at your marketing, sales, and profit goals in Figure 2.5. Try to figure out what it will cost to reach them. If it is more than you can afford, fine. That forces some choices on you. You need a marketing budget that you can live with, one that helps you reach your goals and doesn't tie you to the past or to a formula that can't adjust to sudden shifts.

The best marketing budgets have two parts: first, a fixed monthly amount to meet ongoing, monthly marketing expenses; second, a contingency or project budget to help you meet unexpected marketing needs. A new market may open up, or a competitor retire, or new competition appear. How you respond to these opportunities and challenges is heavily influenced by your budget.

You know your marketing, sales, and profit goals. Discuss these with your accountant or business advisors. Marketing without money is like making bricks without straw. It can't be done without divine intervention—and that kind of marketing help cannot be relied on.

Incomplete campaigns eat profits. Make sure you have enough money to finish your marketing campaigns. You will get tired of your advertisements just about when your markets first take notice of them. That's a problem you can easily deal with. But running out of money is another matter.

To set up your budgets, use your resources. Your accountant or financial advisors can help you put dollar costs to your goals more efficiently than you can. However, you can provide estimates, based on your goals

> Marketing without money is like making bricks without straw.

This is not an exhaustive list. Use it as a starting point. Your company will use some of these categories plus others peculiar to your marketing needs.

1. Selling (direct costs)
   Sales salaries and commissions $ 2,500
   Travel $ 3,800
   Entertainment $ _____
   (marketing database)

2. Selling (indirect costs)
   Training $ 4,500
   Marketing research $ 2,400
   Sales statistics $ 1,000
   Subscriptions and dues $ 600

3. Advertising $ 10,000

4. Sales promotion other than advertising $ 12,000 (direct sales)

5. Public relations $ 600

6. Shipping and handling
   Order filling, packaging $ _____
   Postage and cartage $ 2,400

7. Credits and collection
   Administrative expense $ _____
   Bad debt allowance $ 500

8. Marketing administration $ 1,200

   Total $ 42,000

FIGURE 2.7 Marketing Budget Items

and prior experience in your business. Sketch in your first rough estimates in Figure 2.8.

Fill in Figure 2.8 by listing the marketing actions you plan to take, noting when they will happen, and how much they will cost. Your aim here is simply to get an idea of what would be the best marketing budget for you in light of your plans. You will return to this budget sketch later, and will almost certainly have to modify it in light of new ideas and available cash.

Summary for Chapter Two

- Preliminary goals (personal, marketing, sales, profit) have been established for the next year and the next three years (see Figures 2.3 and 2.5).

Made by:_____ Date:_____

Reviewed by: _____ Date: _____

Goal or Action	Timing	Annual Costs
Yellow pages	annual	$ 2,400
Chamber of commerce	2 ads/yr.	1,200
Brochure		4,000
Mailings	4 times	1,200
Misc. ads	4 times/yr.	750
New services promotion direct mail and telemarketing		12,000
Internet/Web page		3,000
TOTAL:		$24,550

FIGURE 2.8 Preliminary Marketing Budget Estimates

- Some problems have been identified and initial corrective steps taken (see Figure 2.6).
- Your products and services have been listed (see Figure 2.2).
- Target markets have been identified and linked with products and services (see Figure 1.2).
- A marketing budget estimate has been made (Figure 2.8).
  Make copies of Figures 2.2, 2.3, 2.5, 2.6, and 2.8 to refer to in subsequent chapters. Your marketing plan will grow from these initial assumptions and estimates.

  A list of effective small-business marketing strategies is given in Chapter Ten. See Figure 10.3. As you work through the planning process, your strategic choices will begin to emerge.

CHAPTER THREE

PRODUCTS AND SERVICES

If you are already in business, you already have products, services, markets, and problems. If you are about to begin a business, you probably have a clear idea of what you will be selling, where, when, and to whom.

The leading theoretical approach to marketing demands that you first determine what your markets want, then provide a way to satisfy them profitably. That's fine if you have the luxury of choosing your target market and product/service mix before you start a business. Most of us, though, are limited by our experience and interests, to say nothing of other limitations such as money, family obligations, and so forth.

What can you do if you are already in business? Make haste slowly. Change to a marketing orientation, a marketing strategy that focuses on your customers' perceptions and demands. Understand your target

THREE RETAIL IDEAS FROM REI

REI, an outdoor outfitter, in Seattle may offer over 60,000 items in their flagship store, but according to an article in *Fast Company* (December 1997) they offer something more important. Here are three important ideas for retailers.

1. *Sell values, not products.* REI is actually a huge co-op, with 1,400,000 members. These members have a say in how the business is run, receive rebates, and make sure that the company remains true to its core values.
2. *Try before you buy.* REI offers their customers a chance to try out climbing shoes on a rock wall, raingear in an indoor monsoon, or a camp stove in a wind tunnel. Experience sells products.
3. *Live what you sell.* REI is staffed with active outdoor enthusiasts—rock climbers, bike riders, whitewater canoeists. They can relate to the customers because they share the customers' passions.

markets in depth, and measure the products and/or services you offer against the demands of those markets. You can change product and service lines over time to meet the changing demands of your customers and prospects. But don't suddenly switch—it takes planning and time.

There are powerful constraints on the kinds of products and services you can offer: money, time, customer habits, competition, and technology are a few. Creating demand for a new product and changing consumer buying habits is close to impossible. Introducing a new technology can bankrupt you. The number of truly innovative products or services introduced each year is tiny, and beyond the scope of this book.

Most products and services are generic. While you may think your products and services are special, that perception is not necessarily shared by your market.

To gain a competitive advantage, do three things.

1. Know your products and services better than the competition knows theirs.
2. Know the benefits of your products and services from your customers' perspective.

> Creating demand for a new product and changing consumer buying habits is close to impossible.

PRODUCT LIFE CYCLE

Think of your product as having a life cycle that ends when the product is no longer on the market. When you introduce the product, profit isn't the main issue; you try to gain market awareness by promotion and carefully selected channels of distribution. In the growth phase, competition enters the picture and profits increase as the market expands quickly. In the mature phase, sales level off and differentiation strategies take over. This is usually the longest phase as products can often be refreshed, repackaged, and repositioned in order to extend their appeal. Finally the product enters a period of decline where sales taper off, cost cutting becomes common, and the number of competitors decreases.

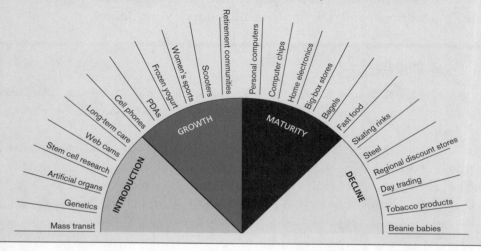

3. Know where your product stands on the "product life cycle." The position on the product life cycle affects pricing as well as sales strategies.

Understand the benefits your customers hope to get from your products or services. Look at your business from their point of view: Without a strong reason to think otherwise, one hardware store is like another; lawyers are interchangeable; seafood markets are where you buy fish. What's so special about your screwdrivers, or wills, or halibut?

People buy benefits. What they want is not necessarily what you think you are selling. They buy solutions to their problems. They buy satisfaction of needs and wants. The solutions and satisfactions are the benefits they buy along with your products and/or services. Benefits are the "what's in it for me?" that your customers seek.

QUESTION 7

What are the benefits of your products and services?

A careful product and service line analysis goes beyond a list of what you currently sell, and far beyond product knowledge. Not that these are unimportant pieces of information—in fact, that's where product/service line analysis begins.

List the products and services you currently sell. (Go back and refer to Figure 2.2.) You may want to reorganize or recategorize your products or services, or add to your list. Enter the products or services on Figure 3.4.

Before you can match up products and/or services and markets, you have to form a clear idea of what needs and wants those products and services satisfy. Any product or service can satisfy a number of wants and needs for the same people. While people don't always know why they buy what they buy, you can draw some useful conclusions by observing and inquiring.

Think of several applications for each product or service, and several sets of wants and needs they satisfy. By communicating this to your target markets, you greatly increase the market appeal of those products and services. The more reasons to buy you can communicate to your target markets the better.

For each product or service, ask: What is its purpose? What needs or wants does it satisfy for your customers? For your prospects? Jot down the most obvious needs and wants each product or service satisfies on Figure 3.2. This will give you a better understanding of the markets you can reasonably target and provide the underpinnings of your marketing strategy.

> Think of several applications for each product or service, and several sets of wants and needs they satisfy.

What kinds of wants and needs should you consider in Figure 3.2? Marketing gurus have listed thousands. A handful are offered in Figure 3.1.

For each product or service: Is it a breadwinner now, or will it be in the future? Is it past its prime? Should it be continued? Or given more support (financial, personnel, promotion)? You want to put your resources to work where they'll have the best long-term payoff. Where is the product or service on its life cycle?

Should you expand current product lines? Sometimes sales of one product reveal customer needs for another—though there are obviously limits to this. If a significant number of your customers ask for a product that would be an extension of your current lines, the risk may be worth taking. It takes less effort to cross-sell to your current customers than it does to create new customers.

Ask product line questions quarterly. It's easy to get so attached to the old product line that we forget to update it. Meanwhile the market moves away.

> *Sometimes sales of one product reveal customer needs for another—though there are obviously limits to this.*

What are the particular advantages/disadvantages of each product or service as compared with competitive products and services? Product/service comparisons tip you off to competitive positioning. In Chapter Five, "Competitive Analysis," further marketing comparisons will help keep you ahead of the competition. For now, take special note of differences in target markets and benefits advertised.

Are you offering the right mix of products and services to meet your customers demands? One way is to check each product or service line against the following form (Figure 3.1) to get a feel for why people might buy that particular product or service. Don't just guess. Ask your customers, focus groups, trade authorities or other sources of information to fill these forms out. Guessing is too dangerous.

Even though individuals ultimately make all purchasing decisions, their approach will differ depending on whether they are buying for themselves or for their company or institution. Several ways of looking at buyer wants and needs are shown here—not to confuse you, but to help you make useful distinctions. Use the blank spaces in the first column to adapt the form to your products and markets. Copy Figure 3.1 and use the copies to analyze your main product or service lines. Any check mark in the "Don't Know" column indicates a need for further research.

"You don't get in trouble buying IBM..." attitude is a good example of bureaucratic thinking. The IBM choice isn't necessarily the best, but it's viewed as defensible.

The next form, Figure 3.2, helps you compare your products or services to those offered by your main competitors. This is one of several ways to focus on your competitive position. Fill this out for each product or service

Basis for Wanting Things

	Applies	Doesn't Apply	Don't Know
To fill biological needs		X	
To gain security	X		
To get status		X	
To gain recognition		X	
To satisfy aggressions		X	
To satisfy sensibilities		X	
To lessen anxiety	X		
To save time	X		

Buyer Motivations

	Applies	Doesn't Apply	Don't Know
Satisfaction of the senses		X	
Imitation of others		X	
Style		X	
Profit	X		
Convenience	X		
Knowledge		X	
Comfort	X		
Fear	X		
Pride		X	
Curiosity		X	
Pleasure		X	
Self-expression or self-actualization		X	
Gaining an advantage		X	
Saving money	X		

Important Buying Factors for Institutional Markets

	Applies	Doesn't Apply	Don't Know
Dependability	X		
Discounts for bulk orders		X	
Price and quality	X		
Relationship with current vendors			X
Customization	X		
Market exclusivity		X	
Value	X		
Delivery schedules		X	
Guarantees			X
Safety for the purchasing agent		X	

FIGURE 3.1 Why Do People Buy Things?

Product/service	Management Consulting	
	Yours	**The Competitions'**
Target markets	small service & retailers, sales $700K-$5M	most are serving the $3M+ businesses
Benefits advertised/promoted	personal service, security, maximize profits, leverage resources, local, fast response	security of using large regional firm, depth of expertise and staff
Quality	x	x
Price	on low side	higher
Improved versions	convenient; will visit	
Location	meet clients, deadlines	ditto
Delivery	excellent	ditto
Follow-up service	very good	good
Availability	location a plus	good
Convenience	good	
Reliability	excellent	good
Service	no satisfaction, no charge	depends on account size
Guarantees	experience with small business owners	?
Other (specify):		not as much

FIGURE 3.2 Product Comparison Form

you offer. For the sake of simplicity, compare only to the leading competitive products or services.

Comparisons are another place you may discover new applications, new product ideas, new opportunities. Look outside your business. Maybe the competition has a wider, deeper, or more specialized line. Would this make sense for your business? Maybe their packaging is better, or their distribution or delivery system is superior. Perhaps their advertising is stronger. Adapt Figure 3.2 to compare product mix, product lines, or other areas where you might be able to gain a competitive edge or blunt a competitive weakness.

Have you made improvements in your products or services lately? Are you planning any? You don't want your products and services to become stale or old-hat, or to be made obsolete by your competitors' changes. This is more than a question of style or fads. "New! Improved!..." is a great marketing line, especially if the product or service is really new and improved. Improvements are a powerful positioning tool: Who doesn't want the improved model?

What new products and services are you planning? Should you develop new ones? Fill out a product line? Meet competition? Or should you prune back your product line to the most profitable elements?

The most powerful marketing strategy for any small business is to locate and dominate market niches too small or too specialized for bigger companies to profitably invade. Quite often this calls for new products, or highly specialized sets of skills. However, any new product or service cries out for strong marketing justification. Otherwise, it's all too easy to squander your resources on exciting but unprofitable new ventures.

What are possible substitutes for your goods or services? Are there any new developments (technological, social, economic) that might result in new ways of satisfying your market's wants and needs?

Not all dangers and opportunities are obvious. The only way to keep abreast of what might affect your business is to read, attend trade or other business shows, and keep alert. Your chances of picking up on an opportunity are far greater than your competitors' if you periodically review and analyze your product and service lines. Refer back to Figure 1.5: SWOT Summary.

List five new applications for your products and/or services. Repackaged products or new applications of old products open up new marketing opportunities. For the product grid (see Figure 3.7), think of new applications as new products.

Huge marketing gains have come from new applications of old products and services. You can sometimes repackage or reposition a product or service to appeal to a wider market, or to a deeper penetration of your

> The most powerful marketing strategy for any small business is to locate and dominate market niches too small or too specialized for bigger companies to profitably invade.

Ask your cus-
tomers, suppliers,
sales force, and
other interested
persons what your
products and ser-
vices might be
used for.

current markets. A classic example of repackaging: Arm & Hammer baking soda sells more widely as a refrigerator cleaner and air freshener than
it ever did as a baking soda.

Ask questions. Ask your customers, suppliers, sales force, and other
interested persons what your products and services might be used for.
Their answers might provide new applications that result in tomorrow's
sales.

Use the answers and ideas you generate to fill out Figure 3.3.

Work with these ideas to rethink how your products might be mar-
keted. As an example, basketballs are used as float valves in some industrial applications. Their features of toughness, uniform size and quality,
roundness, and floatability made them ideal for this purpose.

Product/service __management advisory services__

What are its features? __tax prep. and information (standard); specific industry expertise;__
__like adding a chief financial officer to team__

What benefits does it produce? __helps client grow and make better profits; more__
__financial expertise__

How is it used? __ongoing business planning__

How is it purchased (unit, bulk, with other products)? __retainer (annual) or special project__

What are other possible applications of this product/service? __acquire expertise in other industries__

FIGURE 3.3 Product Application Worksheet

Your Product or Service	Benefits it Offers	Possible Target Markets
	(Wants/Needs Fulfilled)	
1. business consulting	solves business owner's problems	Retail,
2. monthly accounting	keeps books up to date	Manufacturing
3. audits	keeps clients from worrying; saves $$	and
4. tax return preparation	tax return is done correctly	Service Firms
5. tax consultation and representation	keeps clients from worrying; saves $$	with sales of
6. special projects	fulfills client's specific need	$700,000
7. other accounting services	client can have whatever is needed	to $5,000,000

FIGURE 3.4 Product/Service Benefits and Markets

Now put the two concepts together in Figure 3.4. What wants and needs do your products fill? Who might have these wants and needs? What would be the best fit between products and markets?

QUESTION 8

What is the Unique Selling Proposition (USP) of your products and services?

What is the USP for your product and service lines?

What sets your products and services apart from the rest? For each product and service ask: Is it quality? Price? Convenience? Style? Professionalism? Ask the same questions about your store, restaurant, or office. The information gathered in Figure 3.2 is the basis for determining your unique selling proposition.

What sets your products and services apart from the rest?

Your aim is to develop an image or perception in the marketplace that you offer something special. Your neighborhood convenience store has a unique selling proposition: You can get a loaf of bread or a jar of mayonnaise without getting in your car, at odd hours. Look at competing businesses and ask what's special about them. Can those insights help you position and define your business? Every business has something special to recommend it. What's your claim?

You can set your products apart from the competition by looking at the following:

- *New, improved.* Matthew's Teak Cleaner took a messy, dangerous, splattery process and simplified it.
- *Packaging.* Think that L'Eggs profit comes from a superior stocking? Think again. Look at the way cell phones are designed: color inserts, small to very small sizes. The packaging may cost more than the technology.
- *Pricing.* BIC grabbed the ball-point pen market with their 19 cent pen. On the other hand, lack of courage in pricing is a major weakness for small business. Be very careful: Small businesses cannot afford to compete on price. If you do compete on price, aim to be the most expensive, not the cheapest.
- *Advertising and promotion.* What really is the difference between MacDonald's and Burger King? Better yet, think of Frank Perdue and his chickens. Chicken is chicken is chicken—until Frank Perdue changed our perceptions of a commodity and differentiated his product from everyone else's. You pay more for a Perdue chicken, too.
- *Delivery.* Retail stores all over the world are being hurt by direct marketing. It's the fastest growing retail segment. Lands' End, L.L. Bean, Spiegel's, Victoria's Secret, and hundreds of other merchants let you shop at home, and will quickly deliver their products to your door.
- *Convenience.* Look at direct marketing again. Or check out your local 7-11 Store. Even banks are beginning to be open for more convenient hours due to the press of competition. A bank that opens Saturday morning has a big advantage over a bank that doesn't. A bank with many ATMs scattered around their market area offers more than one that doesn't provide such access.
- *Computer-based convenience.* Now you can do all your banking and investing online. You can order books from Amazon or Powell's or Barnes & Noble and have them shipped to you overnight. You can buy clothing from L.L. Bean, Lands' End, or Hanna Anderson, or go shopping at Macy's at 3 AM at <www.macys.com>. Buy French cheese from <www.fromages.com>. Order from a vast catalog of wine at <www.popswine.com>. Get a hand-cranked ice cream maker from <www.lehmans.com>. Still think you don't need to have a Web site?

Your aim is to develop an image or perception in the marketplace that you offer something special.

- *Follow-up service.* After-sale efforts are strong product/service differentiators. Wherever you live, Sears will service your washing machine. Today. That's a deliberate policy—and sharply contrasts with discount stores. Both after-sale service and price chopping are valid marketing strategies. But Sears makes more money in the long run by stressing service, not price. A medical practice that routinely involves its patients in their own health care by sending reminders will lose fewer customers than one that saves money by not keeping in touch.

QUESTION 9

What product or service is the best contributor to your overhead and profits? Your worst?

This is a simple accounting question. If you cannot tell quickly which product you sell makes the most money (net of all expenses, including marketing and sales costs, bad debts and so forth), then you better have a talk with your accountant. This is important information with very direct marketing implications: Where do you make money? Where do you lose money? How can you do more of the former and less of the latter—i.e., Can you ride your strong products more? Cull the losers? Who buys the good products? Who buys the bad ones?

Where do you make money? Where do you lose money?

Products with major impact on O & P:

Contributors	Amounts
1. business consulting	$ 85,000
2. monthly accounting services	$ 45,000
3. audits	$ 20,000
4. tax consult and representation	$ 90,000
5. special projects	$ 60,000
6.	$

Detractors	Amounts
1. individual tax returns	$ <9,000>
2.	$
3.	$
4.	$
5.	$
6.	$

FIGURE 3.5 Winners and Losers

THE BOSTON CONSULTING GROUP'S PRODUCT PORTFOLIO MATRIX

High market growth

Low market growth

High   Market share relative to your competition   Low

Use this matrix as a way to manage your products. You want to cull the dogs, or products with a low share of a low growth market. Problem children have a low share of a fast growth market. Increasing market share may be too costly to justify keeping them.

Stars are products with high market share in a growing market. These are the big revenue generators. Cash cows, or high shares of a slow or declining market, generate cash and require little investment, so you want to keep them as long as they are profitable.

There may be excellent reasons to lose money for a while: gaining market share, acquiring mastery of a new technology or learning new skills, investing today for tomorrow's profits. A current loser is not necessarily a dog or problem child. Nor is a current star necessarily good. You may miss out on an emerging market by sticking with a product too long.

The important point: Know what products and services contribute or take away from your business.

The last piece of the product/service analysis puzzle is to look at Figure 3.6: Product and Strategy Grid. Where do your leading products and services fall on this grid? Your aim is to increase sales and profits. There are four basic ways to do this.

Ask yourself how you could sell old products to new customers, or new products to old customers before even considering selling new products to new customers. Increasing sales of old products to old customers is normally the safest way to increase sales, but may not provide a sufficiently large gain. Selling new products to new customers is as risky as starting a new business—perhaps riskier, because it will sap your energy at the expense of your current business.

All of this chapter leads to Figure 3.7: New Product/Service Objectives. If you decide to make changes in these areas, or want to provide new goodies for your target markets to purchase, treat these changes

Increasing sales of old products to old customers is normally the safest way to increase sales.

	Core Markets	New Target Markets
P **R** **O** **D**	Old product, old customers (lowest risk) Strategy: market penetration	Old product, new customers (risky) Strategy: market development
U **C** **T**	New products, old customers (risky) Strategy: product development	New products, new customers (riskiest) Strategy: diversification

This grid is known as Arsott's Matrix, from a 1957 *Harvard Business Review* Article. If you are planning on growth, this is a useful way to consider your options.

FIGURE 3.6 Product and Strategy Grid

Person responsible: __RM__   Review date: __2/8/03__

Product/Service Idea: __Business management consulting for automobile and equipment dealers__

Benefits it will offer: __Increased profits, financial strategy improvement, depth of our experience__

Target markets: __Automobile dealerships, body shops__

Timing: __12 months__

Anticipated sales: ($ or unit; by quarter) __$10,000/yr. minimum fee__

Anticipated costs:

1. Development: __$5,000 to $10,000__

2. Advertising: __Direct sales, mail__

3. Impact on other products/services: __Will augment client base__

4. Other (specify): _____

Comments: __This is a high growth area due to the nature of the industry__

Action taken: _____

By: __RM__   Date: _____

FIGURE 3.7 New Product/Service Objectives

Product/Service	1st Quarter	2nd Quarter	3rd Quarter	4th Quarter	Total
1. Business consulting					
2. Monthly accounting					
3. Audits					
4. Tax return prep.					
5. Tax consultation and representation					
6. Special projects					
7. Other accounting services					
8.					
9.					

FIGURE 3.8 Summary of Product/Service Goals

Changes that make good business sense should be implemented carefully and systematically, not left to chance.

as seriously as any other major change in your business. Set objectives, including costs, deadlines, and responsibility. Changes that make good business sense should be implemented carefully and systematically, not left to chance.

Use all the information gathered so far to flesh out the form. Consider improved or changed products and services to be new products or services.

Don't hurry with any product change. Let the idea stew for a while. Discuss it. Play the devil's advocate. New products have huge hidden costs that are difficult to foresee, and seldom pay off as well or as fast as you hope.

Summary for Chapter Three

- You looked at your products and services and noted the benefits they offer and the target markets who seek those benefits. Keep a copy of Figure 3.4 for reference. Update it as needed.
- You compared your products and services to those offered by the leading competitors to determine differences and gain preliminary ideas on how to differentiate your business from theirs. Figure 3.2 will help you determine the unique selling proposition of each product or service, which will be used in setting advertising directions.
- You looked at each major product and service to find new applications (and new target markets). Figure 3.3 is a piece of the competitive analysis puzzle, as well as a source of new product line or product mix ideas.
- Risk analysis entered the picture in Figure 3.5. This will be reexamined in Chapter Ten, Strategic Planning.
- One result of product and service analysis is to help you spot competitive strengths and weaknesses in what you market. You will use this in Chapter Five to help define your competitive position.
- New product and service objectives are set in Figure 3.7. You may have to work these into your sales and profit goals. New products cast long shadows.

CHAPTER FOUR

CUSTOMERS AND PROSPECTS

Who wants your goods and services?

You can't know too much about your customers and prospects. This calls for marketing research. Facts and figures elevate your marketing plans from wishful thinking to purposeful action plans. There is no substitute for hard information.

Your hunches, based on experience and observation, are important. They simplify market research by defining limits and setting directions for further investigation.

But they have to be substantiated. Hunches have an irksome way of being half-truths, and half-truths can be disastrous. "I feel that there's a big market for this..." and "I have a hunch that we can double sales by...." are two traps business owners fall into. Put another way, businesses aren't destroyed from outside, by competitors or a malign fate. They self-destruct.

You have to know how your target markets perceive the value of your products and/or services to make good marketing decisions. If you don't know how your company and its products are perceived, you will waste time and aim the wrong products at the wrong markets at the wrong time.

Professional marketing consultants can get this information faster and cheaper than you can. If your budget is tight, check with local business schools. Marketing professors sometimes do consulting work. Since most basic market research questions are the same, this saves you from reinventing the wheel. It should cost you no more than out of pocket expenses. They know the questions to ask and how to get the answers, and they will help you put this information to work. Ferreting out better opportunities for you to pursue is an added bonus for your investment.

> **Y**our hunches, based on experience and observation, are important.

MARKETING RESEARCH SAMPLES

Marketing research provides answers to questions about the entire company such as:

- Who are your best customers and prospects?
- How does the 80/20 rule (that 80 percent of your profits come from 20 percent of your customers) affect you?
- How do they perceive your products and services?
- What do they want from a business like yours?
- How can you satisfy their needs and wants profitably?
- What's the potential of this market for your company?
- Should you market goods, services, or both?
- What do your customers read, watch, listen to?

The following are good sources of marketing research information:

- Customer lists
- Trade publications
- Local trade associations
- Chambers of commerce
- Service clubs such as Rotary or Kiwanis
- Government agencies: economic development agencies, Small Business Administration programs, Department of Commerce
- Libraries, both corporate and public

QUESTION 10

Who are your current customers?

You can't specify target markets, segment the markets, or otherwise improve your marketing abilities without detailed knowledge about your current customers.

What will you do when the next fad hits?

Suppose your market is limited to Britney Spears fans. What will you do when the next fad hits? Grow up with your market and change with them? Cater to the tastes of adolescents forever? If you sell to individual consumers, what are they like? What are the demographics of the market? What are the people's age, gender, income, stage in the life cycle, and education level?

If you sell to industrial markets, what markets are they? Who are the prospective customers? What are their sales levels and geographical distributions? Who makes the buying decision? What market segment buys which products—and what information can these people give you?

Fill in Figure 4.2 for every job you bid on. Over a period of several months this will give you a feel for why you are or are not winning these

BASIC MARKET RESEARCH QUESTIONS

These are a few questions that basic market research will help you answer.

Information about the buyer

- Age?
- Annual income?
- Gender?
- Ethnic group?
- Profession or occupation?
- Owner of a home?
- Media preferred?
- When do they buy?
- How do they buy?
- What do they buy?
- Why do they buy?
- What do they read, watch, listen to?

Information about the competition

- Market share?
- Advertising plan?
- Price strategies?
- Distribution?
- Length of time in business?

Information about the product

- Benefits?
- Price?
- Service?
- Design specifics?
- Where sold?
- Packaging?
- How will it be used?
- How many bought in a year?
- What to improve?

bids; this in turn translates into specific improvements in how you approach industrial or organizational markets. If you have bid on jobs in the past, fill these in retroactively—the results may surprise you.

Market segmentation is a method of organizing and categorizing those persons or organizations that you think will buy your products. Look at

Go through this exercise to gain a preliminary sense of the demographics of your target market. The reason to begin with "your best customers" is simple. Some people are better customers for you than others, and you presumably would want to find more customers like them. You may have a variety of best customers. Fine—go through this exercise for each customer group you feel is valuable to you. Don't dwell too long on this form. You will hone the information as you go along.

If you are a new business owner and have no customers yet, go ahead and imagine who your ideal customer would be.

1. Describe your best customers:
    age
    sex   *men*
    income level
    occupation
    If industrial or business:
    type of business (SIC)   *auto-related*
    size   *$2M-5M in sales*

2. Where do they come from?   ☒ local   ❑ regional
    (check one)   ❑ national   ❑ international
                                    ❑ tourist

3. What do they buy?
    product(s)
    (services)   *—especially management and financial*
    benefits

4. How often do they buy?   ❑ daily   ❑ weekly
    (check one)   ❑ monthly   ❑ every now and then
                                    ☒ other   *annual retainer*

5. How much do they buy?
    Units
    Dollars   *$8,000—$12,000/yr.*

6. How do they buy? (check one)   ❑ credit (you invoice them) ❑ cash
                                    ☒ contract

7. How did they learn about your business?   ❑ advertising: newspaper, radio/TV
    (check all that apply)   ☒ word of mouth   ❑ location
                                    ☒ direct sales   ❑ Internet
                                    ❑ other (specify)

8. What do they think of your
    business/products/services?   *they love it —*
    (Customer perceptions)

9. What do they want you to provide
    (what benefits are they looking for that you   *more comparative data, help contain costs,*
    can or should provide?)   *better knowledge of financial management*

FIGURE 4.1 Who Are Your Customers?

10. How big is your market?
    geographically
    population
    ~~potential customers~~　　　　　　　　　　　*40 auto dealers in immediate area*

11. What is your share of that market?　　　　　*~ 10 percent now*
    (market share)

12. How do you want your markets to perceive your　　*as the experts in running dealerships*
    business?

Examples of Figure 4.1 are given at the end of this chapter.

FIGURE 4.1 Who Are Your Customers?, continued

your customers and note their salient characteristics, then look to wider markets for more groups of people with the same (or similar) characteristics. The usual route is to begin with a fuzzy concept, seek out more detailed information to help define some rough market segments, then

WANT TO SELL TO THE GOVERNMENT?

Do you or can you market your goods and services to the government? The Small Business Administration (SBA) has a valuable Web site for you: <http://pro-net.sba.gov>. What is it? This is taken from their site.

Welcome to Pro-Net!

Pro-Net is an electronic gateway of procurement information—for and about small businesses. It is a search engine for contracting officers, a marketing tool for small firms, and a "link" to procurement opportunities and important information. It is designed to be a "virtual" one-stop procurement shop.

A Search Engine...

Pro-Net is an Internet-based database of information on more than 195,000 small, disadvantaged, 8(a), HUBZone, and women-owned businesses. It is free to federal and state government agencies as well as prime and other contractors seeking small business contractors, subcontractors, and/or partnership opportunities. Pro-Net is open to all small firms seeking federal, state, and private contracts.

Businesses profiled on the Pro-Net system can be searched by SIC codes; key words; location; quality certifications; business type; ownership race and gender; EDI capability, etc.

Government (including local, state and federal) is a huge market. The SBA does a good job of making that market accessible for small businesses.

Project or Bid (by customer)	Product or Service	Won or Lost?	Date	Reasons
101 Auto	consulting	L	Oct.	personality clash
Seacoast Nissan	consulting	still alive	start in May	
Forbes Rolls	consulting	W	April	specific services fit
Honda of Gonic	consulting	W	Feb.	friend recommended us

FIGURE 4.2 Project or Bid Analysis

refine these into better-defined target markets. This can be highly rewarding as well as entertaining.

The ingenuity of market research professionals is noteworthy. As an example, a research technique called VALS (for Value and Lifestyle Study) developed by the Stanford Research Institute helped Manufacturers Hanover Trust Company in New York identify six psychographic groups within one demographic segment—the "baby boomers." (Psychographics, a useful market analysis tool, examines the lifestyles and values of various market segments to determine how consumers think and what motivates them.) The upshot was a successful marketing campaign that used only one slogan, "We realize your potential," to appeal to the six different mindsets. You might be able to benefit from describing your customers and hot prospects using the segmentation criteria in Figure 4.3.

Put these to work for you. Figure 4.4: Market Segmentation Worksheet may be helpful. You will probably find that you sell most profitably (and comfortably) to certain segments and poorly to others, which should affect your planning. Think of the old 80/20 rule: 80 percent of your profits come from 20 percent of your customers. If you can get a good handle on who that profitable 20 percent is and who the unprofitable 80 percent is, you will prosper.

Now look at the major market segments that you currently market to (or intend to market to). First "define" the market segment by product or service. Who is the customer or prospect? How do you describe those persons? For example, you might describe corporate customers by SIC code,

> You will probably find that you sell most profitably (and comfortably) to certain segments and poorly to others.

Use these categories as criteria to describe your customer base. Look for clusters of people described by these criteria; these help direct further marketing efforts. Your descriptions can be general. For example, Age range: 35–65; Gender: both; Income level: $60,000 and up.

Demographic
    Age range   *45–60*
    Gender   *male*
    Income level   *high*
    Occupation   *owner/manager*
    Religion
    Race/ethnic group
    Education
    Social class

Geographic
    Country   *local*
    Region
    State
    County
    City/town
    Size of population
    Climate
    Population density

Psychographic
    Leader or follower   *N/A*
    Extrovert or introvert
    Achievement-oriented or content with the status quo
    Independent or dependent
    Conservative or liberal
    Traditional or experimental
    Societally-conscious or self-centered

Consumer/Behavioral
    Rate of usage
    Benefits sought
    Method of usage
    Frequency of usage
    Frequency of purchase

Business Markets
    Type of business (manufacturer, (retail,) wholesale, service)   *retail auto & equipment dealers*
    Standard Industrial Classification (SIC) Code
    Size of business   *$2M–$5M*
    Financial strength   *excellent*
    Number of employees   *to 110*
    Location   *local*
    Structure
    Sales level
    Special requirements   *detailed industry*
    Distribution patterns

FIGURE 4.3 Basic Market Segmentation Criteria

Market Segment by Product or Service	Customers	Prospects
business consulting	auto dealers, business owners →	
monthly accounting services	mainly individuals →	
audits	mainly individuals →	
tax return preparation	businesses and individuals	focus on business owners
tax consultation and representation	businesses and individuals →	
special projects	auto & equipment dealers →	auto & equipment
other	small retail	local business

FIGURE 4.4 Market Segment Analysis

or size, or membership association; and individual customers by age, income level, educational attainment, or where they live. Don't get hung up on perfection. Any descriptions you select will be revealing and helpful, and you can always copy these forms and do them over (and over again).

WHAT'S WRONG WITH THIS PICTURE?

One afternoon I went to the kitchen to make a pot of coffee. I turned the faucet—and it came off in my hand. Okay, I figured. I'll just scoot downtown and buy a new one. I turned the water off, removed the faulty faucet, and headed downtown. I went into the hardware store, faucet in hand, and was told that it was now 5 o'clock and the store was shutting, but if I hurried to the other source of plumbing fixtures in town I might be accommodated. Off I went, muttering. At the second store a young sales clerk greeted me, looked around, and said he'd serve me. "We shut at 5," he said, "but the boss isn't here."

When do most people go to the hardware store during the week? After work. Yet the owners of both of these stores had complained to me of the unfair competition from the Big Box on the edge of town, which just happens to be open 18 hours a day every day. Is this unusual? No. Many businesses are run for the convenience of the owner, not the customer.

By: __GL__   Date: ____2/10/03____

Product: __All accounting services we offer__

Describe your best customers (or ideal customer) according to the criteria listed in Figures 4.2 and 4.3: __
__Entrepreneurs in their late 30s to early 50s; owners of retail or service firms; auto and__
__equipment dealers with sales of $700,000 to $5,000,000__

Describe their purchasing patterns: __1. Tax preparation is purchased annually. Most sign up in__
__4th quarter, then stay put unless errors are made or service is poor.__
__2. Occasional: business growth or crisis management.__
__3. Consulting is a very sporadic purchase, usually after being satisfied with our tax and__
__"crisis management" skills.__

What makes them the best or ideal customers for this product or service? __They have good ideas__
__and want them implemented. Also, they can pay our $10,000 annual fee.__

FIGURE 4.5 Market Segmentation Worksheet

Now apply these various segmentation criteria to your markets. Make copies of Figure 4.5: Market Segmentation Worksheet, and use them for each of your product or service lines.

QUESTION 11

What are their buying habits?

Who buys what, when, where and why are key pieces of marketing information. If you determine nothing more than the answers to these questions, you will be miles ahead of most of your competitors.

Gather the following basic information on each product, product line, or service you offer:

- Who makes the buying decision?
- What's the size of the sale in dollars?
- How many units are sold?
- What is your cost per sale?
- What do your customers buy?
- When do they buy it?
- Is their purchase seasonal?
- Why do they buy it?

- Where do they make the buying decision?
- How do they finance their purchase?

How do your customers view your products and services? This is a key research and development question. If you can understand your products from their point of view, you can discover new ways to market your products and services, new target markets, and new profitability. For instance, if a customer has asked for a refinement of a standard product in your line, can you redesign and repackage that product for other people?

As examples of how powerful a marketing tool reworking your basic products and services to fit customer demands can be, think of

- blister packaging of foods and medicines after the first Tylenol scare.
- the evolution of Personal Digital Assistants (PDAs) that can now keep you connected with your e-mail, access your office computer, and double as a beeper and telephone.
- overnight package delivery. Federal Express spotted a market for overnight small package and letter delivery. It was always there; they just were the first to spot it. Their competitors are still playing catch-up.
- cash management accounts opened huge markets for Merrill Lynch. That product should have been developed by the banking industry. However, the bankers were too dumb to notice that their customers' problems juggling various banking and brokerage accounts had created a mammoth opportunity.

The key marketing point: People buy solutions to problems. They buy satisfaction of their wants and needs. They *don't* buy products and services. If your customers have complaints, find out why. What's their problem? How can your company help them solve that problem?

> The key marketing point: People buy solutions to problems.

QUESTION 12

Why do they buy your goods and services?
Answer this one correctly and become rich and famous.

How can you find out why people buy from you? Ask them. Figure 4.6 is a survey that R.C. Montville is using to better understand their corporate clients. It helps if you give your customers a structured survey to work with. This is an area where a professionally developed survey pays off. Call your local SBA office and ask for the nearest Small Business Institute program. Check with local colleges—a customer survey is one of those projects that costs you little and gains you much.

When you do a survey make sure to get answers to these three basic questions:

1. Where did you hear of our store/product/service?
2. What would you like us to offer?

To our valued clients:

Please take a few minutes to complete this short questionnaire. Out aim is to give you the service you need, want, and deserve. Your honest answers to these questions can help us serve you better.

1. How would you rate the quality of work we have performed for you in the past?

   Excellent ＿＿　　　　　　　Good ＿＿　　　　　　Fair ＿＿　　　　　　Poor ＿＿

   1a. If not excellent, please explain.

   ＿＿

   ＿＿

2. How would you rate the timeliness of the work we perform for you?

   Excellent ＿＿　　　　　　　Good ＿＿　　　　　　Fair ＿＿　　　　　　Poor ＿＿

   2a. If not excellent, please explain.

   ＿＿

   ＿＿

3. What service would you like us to perform for you that we do not offer?

   ＿＿

   ＿＿

4. Please feel free to give us any constructive criticism you feel we could use.

   ＿＿

   ＿＿

5. We plan to begin a seminar series in the not too distant future. What areas would you like to see covered in these seminars?

   ＿＿

   ＿＿

   5a. How interested would you be in attending our seminars?

   Very ＿＿　　　　　　Somewhat ＿＿　　　　　Little ＿＿　　　　Not at all ＿＿

FIGURE 4.6 R.C. Montville and Company's Client Survey

3. How can we serve you better?

In Chapter Three, Figure 3.1, you matched products with the needs and wants that they fulfill. Now put those insights to work. Who has these needs and wants? Which of your target markets can you satisfy profitably? Maybe you can reposition some of your products to appeal to these markets. Maybe you will have to change the product/service mix.

Keep in mind that people won't buy goods and services they don't want, no matter how good the advertising and positioning. You can only sell them what they want to buy. Sometimes that will be what they need. But it will very seldom be what you think you are selling.

Some examples: You think you sell a medical service. Your customers think they are buying a solution to a problem, a friendly ear, an antidote to fear. Charles Revson was widely quoted as saying that while his factories made perfume, he sold hope. Detroit sells transportation, not cars. Hollywood sells entertainment, not movies. Disneyland sells happiness.

More examples: If you sell to bureaucrats, remember that their number one concern is to be safe. If you sell to teenagers, remember they need to be in step with their peers. If you sell to a local retail customer base, remember they buy convenience, safety, cleanliness, familiarity and courtesy along with your groceries or dry goods.

Apply this way of thinking to your business. What emotional needs or wants do your products satisfy? What other benefits do they provide? Then match those benefits to your target markets.

How can you determine your market's needs and wants? Ask them. Observe them. Read—trade magazines are full of articles about why people buy and what triggers their purchasing decisions. Attend trade seminars. Talk with other business owners and managers. Above all, ask your customers, whether prospective, current or former.

What emotional needs or wants do your products satisfy?

Who are your best customers and prospects?

Use a straightforward approach: Match the information about the most profitable products with the market segments who purchase those products. If you can figure out why they made these purchases, and can find other groups with similar characteristics, in sufficient numbers, then these new groups become your best prospects. With work, they will turn into your best customers.

This is an endless process. Your target markets will change over time; your product lines and mix will change; and your business will change.

But the basic five-step process remains constant.

1. Identify your profitable products and services, including those which will be profitable in the future.
2. Find out as much as you can about the people who buy those products and services. Who are they? What are their buying patterns? How often do they buy? How much do they spend? What offers do they respond to?
3. Find other people like them. These are your hot prospects.
4. Identify unprofitable products, especially those that take up a disproportionate amount of time and money. These are often either "owner's ego" products, products that management has a special investment in, or old familiar products that have outlived their useful life.

CUSTOMER SERVICE AND PLANNING

Truly good customer service comes from paying close attention to details.

The only way I know to do this is to make your customers a component of every business decision, from product, service, location, and pricing issues to staffing and training. While putting customers at the heart of all decisions is extraordinarily tough for large companies, it works well for small businesses. That isn't to say it's easy for small businesses—just much easier than for big ones.

An effective customer service strategy cannot be implemented until you know what your business can and cannot do. You can't just say "I will run a customer centered business" and do it. Your strategy and business evolve together, posing unexpected challenges. The culture of your business, the norms and values and expectations that you and your employees (and to a great extent suppliers and markets) share, change. Above all, your customers' perceptions of your business and the competition never stay still.

Customers come and go. They move, change their buying habits, are lost to competitors. A good working rule of thumb is that your customer base will change at least 20 percent each year—that is, you can expect to have to replace one customer in five every year, and each year there are new products and services to contend with, new shifts in the economy, new competitors. The basic parts of your strategy should remain relatively constant, but many of the details must be continuously updated. Since you sell to a shifting set of customers, you can count on their perceptions of the value of your products and services to shift as well.

What does this mean for you, the business owner? Two key points:

1. You have to continuously engage in market research. You have to know what their perceptions are, what they seek, and how they want to be served.

2. Your plans—business, financing, marketing and personnel plans—all hinge on this ongoing market research. As your market shifts, so should your plans.

5. Find out who buys these unprofitable products and services—and stop marketing to them, or switch them to more profitable products. This may mean leaving a comfortable market for a profitable one. Remember why you're in business: to create and satisfy your customers, at an acceptable profit.

QUESTION 14

What is your market share?

Market share is your percentage of total sales to a given market. For example, if you sell $225,000 worth of medical services annually to a market which buys $1,000,000 worth of that particular service a year, you'd have a 22.5 percent market share. Market share can be measured in unit sales: 225,000 units out of a total market of 1,000,000 units. Or in purchasing units: 225,000 people out of the total market of 1,000,000 buy your product.

By: __RM__   Date: __2/10/03__
Reviewed by: _____   Date: _____

These are our most valuable customers and prospects, ranked from the top. Make sure you list the market segments and their criteria.

Name of Customer	Market Segment	Criteria (Figure 4.3)
1. Forbes Rolls-Royce	auto	$5M sales
2. Honda of Gonic	auto	$3M sales
3. Wheely Honda Cycle Co.	motorcycle	$1.6M sales
4.		

We should target these prospects

Name of Prospect	Market Segment	Criteria (Figure 4.3)
1. Seacoast Nissan	auto	$3M sales
2. So. Me. Harley-Davidson	motorcycle	$2.5M sales
3.		
4.		

We should consider these market niches:
1. Heavy equipment dealers
2. RV dealers
3. Motorcycle dealers
4. Auto parts dealers?

Our customer/prospect objectives for the next year are:
1. Penetrate auto-related markets
2. Upgrade customer list
3. Focus!

FIGURE 4.7 Customer/Prospect Summary Form

Note that market share presupposes knowledge of the total size of the market, which depends in turn on how you define your target market.

Market share information helps you decide whether to enter, abandon, invade, or protect a market niche. As a rule of thumb, a 25 percent market share is dominant, and makes you a major player in that market. If you can identify a market niche large enough for profitability, yet small enough to be unattractive to big businesses—and grab 25 percent of that market, you have a winner. On the other hand, if your archrival has 50 percent of that market, there might not be room for both of you.

QUESTION 14A

Is your market share growing, shrinking, or stable?

QUESTION 14B

Is the market itself growing, shrinking, or stable?
Is it changing in other ways?

A declining market may be a good one to bail out of, or may present a terrific niche possibility. The Underwood Company, makers of deviled ham and other canned meat spreads, has done very well in a market that was vanishing. A growing market may be an opportunity for you to develop a growing niche. It could also present an enticing market to a large company which could swamp the market. Think of what happened when IBM spotted the success of the microcomputer industry.

Market-share information is one of many factors involved in these kinds of strategic choices. You have to use your judgment. Judgment based on facts beats guesswork.

> A declining market may be a good one to bail out of, or may present a terrific niche possibility

Summary for Chapter Four

- You have segmented your customer base (see Figure 4.4).
- You know (based on your research) why these people buy your products or services, and what needs or wants they satisfy.
- This helps you form a clear, easily communicated description of the target markets to which you can effectively market.
- You can now set realistic target market objectives to include in your marketing plan, including the size of your markets, your market share goals, and other precise measures of performance. Fill out Figure 4.6.

  Sample objectives might be to enter some niches, try to attract certain market segments while dropping efforts to attract others, or work on certain product lines that sell to current customers. You have to remember your own business situation and that these objectives are based on analysis, not wishful thinking.

CHAPTER FIVE

COMPETITIVE ANALYSIS

In Chapter Two, Question 5 you made a preliminary list of obstacles that might impede achieving your goals. One of the biggest impediments is the competition. No business operates in a competitive vacuum. There are plenty of smart business owners looking to your target markets for their next sale.

Business is competitive. Customers' needs and expectations shift. New products and different services fight for their dollar. New competitors enter the market while others leave it.

What can you do about the competition? Plenty. Think of the comprehensive scouting reports that major league managers rely on. They carefully observe their competitors. They study everything about them that could possibly affect the outcome of a game. They know who the players are, what their strong and weak points might be, what strategies they use, what they tend to do in a pinch, what resources they can call on, and other information. You need at least as much information about your competitors.

Competitive analysis is an important part of your marketing plan. You can learn from your competitors and strengthen your business. You can predict their plans if you observe them closely. This takes work and close attention to detail. Most small-business owners approach competitive analysis haplessly. Set up a structured approach (think of major league baseball again) and seize a whopping competitive advantage.

> You can learn from your competitors and strengthen your business.

QUESTION 15

Who are your competitors?

Anyone who sells similar products/services in your marketplace, or similar products/services in other marketplaces, or who could sell similar products/services, is a competitor. You compete for your target market's time and money. In the advertising cliché, you want to gain their Attention, Interest, Desire, and Action (the mnemonic is AIDA)—but so do a lot of competing businesses.

Competitive analysis begins with identifying your immediate competition: Who are your five leading competitors?

As you fine-tune your analysis of the competition, you will want to add the less direct competition.

Future competitors may be the most threatening if you are in a highly desirable, rapidly growing market. But for most small-business owners, just staying on top of the current market will be enough.

Remember: You aren't the only smart business owner out there. If you can learn from your competitors, they can learn from you.

You have to learn a lot about your competition before you can make useful comparisons. Remember the big league scouting reports. A scout will follow a team for weeks, making copious observations on each player. Can he hit a curve? How about the shortstop's ability to go to his left? Do they use the hit-and-run, or prefer sacrifice bunts in the late innings? The scouting is organized, thorough, and professionally executed. Otherwise it's not particularly informative.

Business is competitive, and you have to scout out the competition. This may seem like spying. It is. A spy has to have some idea of his or her objectives. So do you. This information sets your marketing strategies.

> **F**uture competitors may be the most threatening if you are in a highly desirable, rapidly growing market.

By: __RM__   Date: __2/11/03__

My closest competitors are

1. __Bridge & Silverman__
2. __S, B & R__
3. __Purdy, Bernstein__
4. __GBS__
5. _____

Other competitors (include indirect and potential competitors) are

1. __Bigelow & Company__
2. __"Big Four" accounting firms__
3. __Major regional firms (acct.)__
4. _____
5. _____

FIGURE 5.1 List of Competitors

Prepared by: <u>GL</u>   Date: <u>2/11/03</u>

Competitor: <u>S, B & R</u>

Product/service: <u>tax preparation and accounting services</u>

Location(s):   <u>Portsmouth</u>

Specific information

     Years in business: <u>24</u>

     Number of employees: <u>20</u>

     Dollar sales: <u>$3,000,000</u>

     Unit sales: _____

     Market share: <u>approximately 20 percent</u>

     Financial strength: <u>excellent</u>

     Profitability: <u>?</u>

Players (include their ages, experience in this business, training or education, business strengths and weaknesses, and other pertinent information)

     President/owner: _____

     Key employees: _____

     Management capability: _____

The competition's marketing strategy

     Key customers: _____

     Major products or services: _____

     Quality: _____

     Image: _____

     Pricing: <u>accounting services: low taxes: high</u>

     Advertising themes: <u>none</u>

     Promotion/public relations efforts: _____

Significant changes (new people, products, etc.): _____

How this competitor competes with you: <u>more conservative</u>

Comments: <u>I need to do more research to finish this!</u>

FIGURE 5.2 Competitor Information

Use Figure 5.2: Competitor Information to organize your scouting reports. Much of the information is readily available from Dun & Bradstreet and other publicly available reports. Your banker can get this information for you, or you can piece it together yourself. Fill in these forms for each serious competitor, and keep the forms on file. Over a year or so you will develop a most informative dossier on your competition.

This is an area where knowledge really is power. For many of us, the problem is gaining that knowledge. There are few shortcuts—but the process is simple enough. You build the dossier piece by piece, over time, using the competition's advertising, press releases, promotional materials of all kinds, your own observations, comments from vendors, customers, employees, friends, and your core of business advisors. As the file grows, you will know enough about your competitors to anticipate their moves, learn from their strengths and weaknesses, and increase your competitive advantage.

Don't feel badly about doing this. Your stronger competitors are doing this to you already.

QUESTION 16

What do your competitors do better than you?

QUESTION 17

What do you do better than your competitors?

Do your competitors see a weakness in your business or a market potential you missed? Your top competitors look at your business for ideas. Do the same to theirs. Your aim is to find out how you stack up against your competition. What are their strengths vis-a-vis yours? Where do you differ?

Smart business owners go beyond scouting the competition. They have themselves scouted ("shopped") in order to have an unbiased appraisal of how they measure up against the competition.

You might want to raise the following questions:

> **Y**our top competitors look at your business for ideas.

- How are your competitors financed?
- Can they raise more money? A division of a larger company, for example, has a potential advantage over a small business in this area.
- Are they heavily in debt? This would make price competition dangerous to them.
- Are they investing in new products or services? Why? (Or why not?)
- What training do they give their personnel? Small-business owners are notoriously unwilling to provide adequate training. This can be exploited.
- What image (if any) are they trying to develop?
- What are their target markets?
- Do they compete on price, quality, service, or convenience?

One application of Figure 5.2 is to alert you to your strengths and weaknesses relative to their business.

Maybe they have a better product, or a more motivated sales force, or better cost and quality controls that result in a price advantage. Maybe they have a superior location or a better distribution system. Or perhaps they are instituting a strong sales training program.

Once you know what their strengths are, learn from them. You don't necessarily want to emulate them—but it makes sense to do so if copying their strengths fits in with your own plans. Avoid their weaknesses in your own business, but be ready to attack them with your marketing strategies. There usually is little difference between one business and another. Those little differences, though, separate the profitable, enjoyable businesses from struggling businesses.

Use Figures 5.3 and 5.4 as guidelines.

In Figure 5.3: Comparing Yourself to Competitors, write down what your competition is doing in the five principal comparison areas. Then, in the last column, jot down how you stack up in these areas. If at all possible, get customer and prospect input on this comparison. Their ideas will almost surely differ from yours, and as frequently noted, there is no substitute for asking your customers and prospects for their help.

The other yardsticks might be product lines, staffing, sales practices, finances, management, or whatever you find to be important competitive information for your business. You have to know how you compare on the other listed items to differentiate your company from the competition.

All five major yardsticks are far more detailed than you may at first think. For example, consider advertising.

Look carefully at all of the competitor's advertising. What are they trying to say? Do they feature price, delivery, or reliability? Do they focus on one strength—for example, technical skill or convenience? How

Look carefully at all of the competitor's advertising.

Prepared by: RM   Date: 2/11/03

Competitor: S, B & R

	Describe Your Competitor's	How Do You Stack Up?
Price	High	Lower, but headed up
Quality	OK	Even better
Service	OK	Even better
Location	Good	Poor—we are changing to a better one
Advertising	None	Aggressive
Other yardsticks	Been around a long time	Relatively new

FIGURE 5.3 Comparing Yourself to Competitors

	Competitor Offers	**We Offer**
Customer seeks:		
Quality		
Exclusivity		
✓Lower prices		Ours lower than competition
Product line		
✓Product service	Depends on size of account	More handholding
Reliability		
✓Delivery		Always meet deadlines
✓Location	Downtown	Easy access & will visit clients
✓Information	Newsletter	News releases and seminars
✓Availability		Always when needed, incl. eves. and weekends
Credit cards		
Credit line		
✓Warranty		If not satisfied, client pays no fee
✓Customer advice		Always provided
Accessories		
✓Knowledgeability		Take courses every year
Polite help		

FIGURE 5.4 Quick Comparison

important do you think their advertising points are to the targeted market? Where do they advertise—trade journals? Radio or newspaper? Billboards? Is their advertising more effective than yours? Should you review your advertising?

Figure 5.4: Quick Comparison provides a list of comparisons based on what your customers are looking for. If you have been listening to your

market, this can provide valuable insights for your marketing strategies—
and provide more ways to differentiate your business from the others.

Your marketing strategy should be based on your strengths, the competition's weaknesses, and the market's desires.

Shore up weak areas in your business to become more competitive.
This can pay off fast. For example, if analysis shows that you have surly
clerks and a dingy store, while the competitors have trained their clerks
to be polite and provide a clean, well-lighted, spacious store, your first
move would be to clean house. The next step would be to advertise the
change widely, and build on whatever strengths you originally had.
Think of how the auto parts industry changed in response to competitive
pressures from large stores such as Sears and Kmart. The mechanic's
macho havens are on the way out, and newer stores (ADAP for one) have
carved out a highly profitable niche by changing the image of auto parts
stores.

> Shore up weak
> areas in your
> business to
> become more
> competitive.

QUESTION 18

What is your competitive position?

Locate yourself on the competitive continuum in Figure 5.5. A visual
reminder of where you are helps stimulate and motivate your employees
the same way that knowing your position in a league helps you knuckle
down to improve your own skills.

Use Figure 5.6: Competitor Analysis Summary to pull all your information about your competition into one place. The number of competitors

MICHAEL PORTER'S FIVE FORCES ANALYSIS

Michael Porter's Competitive Strategy: Techniques for Analyzing Industries and Competitors sets the gold
standard for understanding the centrality of competition in your strategic planning.

His famous five forces analysis looks at the following:

1. What is the threat of entry of new competitors? What are the barriers to entry that might protect
   you? What are the switching costs? Is entry becoming easier?
2. What is the bargaining power of your customers?
3. What is the bargaining power of your suppliers?
4. What substitutes for your products are (might become) available?
5. What is the level of competition in your industry?

This topic is too rich to try to understand from this sketchy introduction. Check out Porter's book (or buy
it for under $30). It's a powerful source of ideas for all businesses, no matter what their size.

	Strong	+		–	Weak

Where are you located on this continuum? What are you going to do about it?
How do you rank relative to the competition in these areas? A '+' means you are stronger than the competition, a '–' means you are weaker.

	Strong	+	–	Weak
Management				
Finances			–	
Marketing			–	
Pricing		+		
Selling		+		
Production		+		
Distribution				
Training			–	
Personnel			–	
Style/image				
Other				

FIGURE 5.5 Competitive Continuum

is arbitrary—but it is important and valuable for you to have a clear understanding of what the other companies pursuing your markets are up to.

Now sum it all up. What do you want to do to improve your competitive position? Ask all of your interested constituencies to help with this: employees, vendors, bankers, and investors all will have ideas you can use. How have others improved their competitive position in areas similar to your weaknesses? Your competitive objectives in Figure 5.7 become the foundations of your competitive strategies: "This is what we want to accomplish and this is how we will do it—by building on our strengths" is a tough strategy to beat.

These objectives don't need to be detailed here. You will be considering other aspects of your competitive position before writing your final marketing plan, and while these preliminary objectives are very important indicators for your planning, you will substantially modify them in the following chapters.

What do you want to do to improve your competitive position?

Competitor:	#1 BS	#2 SBR	#3 PB	#4 GBS
Sales in $	$1.5M	$3M	$1M	$125K
Market share	10%	20%	7%	1%
Product lines				
Service lines	tax, MAS	tax, MAS	MAS	tax, MAS
Reputation	excellent	excellent	good	unknown

FIGURE 5.6 Competitor Analysis Summary

Prepared by: ___RM___ Date: ___2/11/03___

Reviewed by: _____ Date: _____

We need to improve our competitive position in the following areas:

1. _finances_
2. _marketing_
3. _training and personnel_

We can build on our competitive strengths in the following areas:

1. _selling_
2. _production_
3. _personnel_

We can attack our competition in the following weak areas:

1. _service_
2. _offer business consulting in addition to accounting services_
3. _____

FIGURE 5.7 Competitive Objectives

Summary for Chapter Five

- You listed and analyzed your closest competitors, and took note of indirect or potential competition for your markets.
- You have begun to collect detailed information on them (see Figures 5.1 and 5.2).
- You know your relative competitive position, based on a careful assessment of your leading competitors (see Figure 5.5).
- You looked at the comparative strengths and weaknesses of your competition and your own business, with an eye towards improving your competitive position (Figures 5.3 and 5.4).
- This gives you the information to set realistic and attainable competitive objectives for the next year. Figure 5.6: Competitive Objectives summarizes these goals. You will refer back to Figure 5.6 in your marketing plan.

CHAPTER SIX

PRICE SETTING

Three of the most important (and difficult to establish) pieces of your marketing plan are price (how to set prices to maximize profits and achieve other goals), location (where you do business—including distribution patterns), and sales practices (how you sell your products).

Within limits, these are fixed. Prices are somewhat determined by market conditions and competition. Where you open shop is already established, but can be changed. Distribution patterns and delivery routes depend on sales patterns and customer demand. Sales practices are perhaps the hardest patterns to change, and cause the most problems.

However, you do have some latitude in each of these areas. You don't have to play follow-the-leader, or put up with an inadequate location or inept sales practices. You can change them to your benefit and competitive advantage.

> Sales practices are perhaps the hardest patterns to change, and cause the most problems.

QUESTION 19

How do you establish prices?

The dilemma is whether to aim for high volume/low prices (the Wal-Mart route) or low volume/high prices (à la Tiffany's). Wal-Mart's enormous purchasing power, backed by its innovative distribution system, makes them the premier low-cost leader in retail. A few other big box category killers have set the pace in narrower fields following Wal-Mart's model. Office Max and Staples are hard to beat. Home Depot, Wal-Mart's cousin, Sam's Club, and a few other warehouse clubs are successful, while smaller regional discounters have fallen by the side of the road. There can only be one low-cost supplier in any field, and it's a particularly tough role to maintain since the low-cost position is so obvious.

Price setting is complicated by the way your markets react to price changes. Sensitivity to price changes is called "price elasticity." Does a small price rise lead to a large drop in unit sales (price is "elastic"), or does a big price rise lead to a negligible drop in unit sales (price is "inelastic")? Price elasticity studies are frequently available through industry or trade associations. If your trade association doesn't have such studies, try sampling small segments of your markets. Your local college may be able to conduct an elasticity study for you, which has the additional benefit of shielding you from customers who may be highly price sensitive. Students conducting surveys can get more information than your business in these sensitive areas.

All pricing policies are competitive. Knowing how sensitive your target markets are to price changes puts you at an advantage over firms who follow a reactive pricing policy, but there are many other factors to keep in mind.

To set your pricing policy, follow a five step process.

1. Define your pricing objectives.

Tie these to your overall marketing and business goals (see Figures 2.3 and 2.5).

Some common pricing objectives include maintaining or building market share, maximizing profits or return on investment, meeting competition,

> **A**ll pricing policies are competitive.

PRICING STRATEGIES

A convenient way to look at pricing strategies is to use the quality/price matrix.

	Low Quality	High Quality
Low price	Economy	Market penetration
High price	Skim the cream	Premium pricing

Premium pricing is exemplified by Rolls Royce. The customer is willing to pay what is acknowledged to be a premium price in exchange for a superior product and attendant status benefits.

Economy pricing is often seen in commodities; the house brands of cereals and other grocery staples are an example. Perceived quality is secondary to the savings.

Market penetration—think of loss leaders—sets a low price to gain market share rapidly. Who can resist a bargain?

Skimming is the opposite of market penetration. Here the price is set high at first to maximize profits while the product is unique or competitively advantaged.

PRICING FACTORS

Price = Image + Service + Product + Overhead + Profit + Risk

The following factors influence pricing policies:

- *Perceived value to customer.* (Perceived value to customers involves the product plus intangibles such as service, quality, and specialized expertise.)
- *Price sensitivity* (elasticity).
- *Quality.* High quality and higher prices often go together.
- *Product differentiation.* High differentiation and high prices; low differentiation (commodity products) and low prices, often go together.
- *Competition.* Competitive markets and price chopping as a market share strategy go together.
- *Service.* The more service you provide, the higher the price you can charge. A fully assembled, carefully chosen bicycle from a cycle shop costs more than the same bike, disassembled, from an outlet store.
- *Location.* Stores on Rodeo Drive command higher prices than stores in the local strip mall.
- *Target markets.* Some markets buy on price. A low price can scare people off ("The price is so low—what's wrong with this ?") or be an excellent marketing tool. Know your markets.
- *Marketing objectives.* Are you looking for market share? Profits? New markets? Your objectives must be reflected in your price strategies.
- *Your business costs.* Your pricing has to reflect your business, not someone else's.

introducing new products, and increasing sales. Or objectives can include all of these.

Make your pricing objectives explicit. Figure 6.1 helps structure your objectives. Fill it in for each major product line or service. Your aim here is to establish a pricing policy, not to set prices on every single little item you might sell.

2. Establish price ranges.

This is complicated, so call in your accountant or financial advisors. Three questions to raise when setting price ranges are:

- *What is your breakeven point?* (See Figure 6.2.) This establishes the low end of the acceptable range. You must at least meet your expenses (break even) before you can make a profit. Can you reach your breakeven point given sales forecasts and current prices? How far can you exceed it?
- *What are your profit goals?* If you can't reach the profit goals given unit sales forecasts and acceptable prices, rethink your strategies, or market more aggressively. See Figures 2.5 and 3.9.
- *How do your target markets perceive your products/services?* This includes questions of price elasticity as well as product differentiation. Oddly

Make your pricing objectives explicit.

By: _____   Date: _____

Product or service: _____ MAS _____

My Pricing Objectives	What Objective Will Accomplish	Time Frame for Reaching Objective
1. remain competitive	profits and market share	keep on doing as we've been doing
2.		
3.		
4.		
5.		

FIGURE 6.1 Pricing Objectives

enough, the small business scourge "lack of courage in pricing" often stems from not knowing how the market perceives the value of products and services. Don't guess here. Use surveys, questionnaires, market research, and trade studies. Knowledge beats guesswork every time. This piece of knowledge helps you establish the upper limit of your price range. Sometimes this is called "what the market will bear."

Breakeven analysis pinpoints where revenue equals total costs. To calculate your breakeven point, take your most current income statement and

LACK OF COURAGE IN PRICING

This is an especially important consideration for small businesses trying to sell services to other businesses. Some years ago my company was trying to persuade Chase Manhattan Bank in New York to subscribe to our small business management newsletter, *Common Sense*. We offered what we thought was quite a bargain: reprint rights to 12 issues a year for $1,200. We got nowhere. Frustrated, I was complaining about this problem to Jim Howard, the founder of Country Business Services in Vermont (a leading business brokerage). "Go back to see them again," Jim bellowed. "Tell them the price has gone up to $12,000 a year." I protested. "Lack of courage in pricing," Jim roared, now in full spate. "That's your problem. Raise your price. You'll see."

He was right. The vice president we dealt with wasn't a bit shocked. Instead, as he reached for his pen, he told me, "You finally value your products."

Think about it. If you don't put a premium on your time and effort, why should the market buy at any price?

identify each cost as either fixed or variable. Fixed costs are independent of sales level, while variable costs rise and fall with sales. Mixed costs involve elements of both. Most costs will fall readily into fixed or variable. For those that don't, allocate 50 percent to fixed costs, 50 percent to variable.

Fixed Expenses	**Variable Expenses**
Salaries	Sales commissions
Payroll tax	Sales tax
Benefits	Boxes, paper, etc.
Utilities	Travel
Licenses and fees	Freight
Insurance	Overtime
Advertising	Bad debt
Legal and accounting	
Depreciation	**Mixed**
Interest	Telephone
Maintenance and cleaning	Postage

Fixed costs are independent of sales level, while variable costs rise and fall with sales.

Figure 6.3: Price Range Guidelines is useful in at least two ways. First, it gathers a lot of information together in one place—which makes it easier for you to use the information in making pricing decisions. Second, the form helps you look at the forces that drive your pricing policies. You will have to adapt this for a service business (such as the one in the example).

Inventory turn rates (see numbers 3 and 4) need some explanation. They directly affect your profitability. All things being equal, higher turn rates permit lower prices, while lower turn rates go with higher priced items. A grocery turns its produce at least 52 times a year; a jewelry store might profitably have less than one turn a year. Since turn rates have such a strong impact on how you run your business, keep up with trade information and check with your accountant.

The breakeven formula is:

$$BE = F/(S-V)$$

where   BE = breakeven sales in dollars

F = fixed costs in dollars

S = sales expressed as 100%

V = variable costs as a percentage of sales.

If F = $10,000, S = 100%, and V = 50%, Then BE = ($10,000/50%) = $20,000.

In other words, costs will exceed revenue until you have sold $20,000 worth of goods.

FIGURE 6.2 Breakeven Analysis

By: ___GL_____   Date: ___2/12/03_____

Product/service: ___All accounting services_____

Price range: $ __60/hr___ to $ __125/hr___

1. Price floor:
   (a) Markon (gross margin) is _____% of retail price.
   (b) Manufacturer's Suggested Price is $ _____.
   (c) Fixed costs are $ _____. Variable costs are $ _____
       or _____ percent of sales.
   (d) Breakeven is $ _____.

2. Special considerations for this product's price are:
   ☒ service   *Something to think about: Our fees can be higher if clients'*
   ❏ status   *perception of value is raised!*
   ☒ quality
   ❏ loss leader
   ❏ demand
   ❏ product life
   ❏ overhead
   ❏ downtime
   ❏ competition
   ❏ market penetration costs
   ❏ other (specify):

3. Turnover rate is _____ times per year.   *not applicable*

4. Industry turn average is _____ times per year.   *not applicable*

5. Going rate is _____*$50 to $100/hr.*_____.

6. I estimate _____ units will be sold.   *not applicable*

7. ___31___ ~~(number of units)~~ at $ _75/hr._ will cover my fixed costs.
   hours/week

8. Top price possible is $ ____ . (This estimate is based on the customer's perception of value.)

Comments _____

_____

_____

_____

FIGURE 6.3 Price Range Guidelines

In Going Rate (number 5) note what your competitors are charging. This is vital information for service businesses where lack of courage in pricing often leads to undercharging for services. Whenever possible, aim for the top price (see number 8.) You can always back down—but raising a published rate presents special selling problems.

3. Define competitive pricing strategy.

See Figure 6.4 for some ideas. Since all pricing strategies are competitive, a major factor in your choice will be what the other guys are doing. This doesn't mean you want to follow them. It does mean you want to know what they are doing so you can defeat them in the marketplace.

4. Consider the impact of product lines, inventory costs, and selling costs.

Sometimes you have to flesh out a product line to meet other competitive pressures and rather than carry the product forever, you decide to turn it over even at a loss. Inventory costs are a hidden burden on many retail businesses (ask your accountant) and can drive up your short-term borrowing needs.

Some businesses find that sales costs are the dominant pricing factor. Think of life insurance sales, where everyone from the insurance agent on up gets a commission. The premium is based on a minimal product cost, plus a substantial administrative cost, plus a staggering sales cost.

Keep your costs in mind when setting prices. Your price strategies have to reflect your business's cost structures and profit goals, not someone else's.

5. Choose a flexible pricing strategy.

Every industry has its own favorite pricing strategy, and you should use your industry pattern as a guide.

The main methods are:

- *Suggested or going rate*. This is the least defensible method, since it removes your business from the pricing decision. This is far and away the most common method: It is simple. It takes no work. It also is almost totally ineffective.

- *Full cost pricing*. Full-costing may be appropriate if you can identify all your operating costs, then distribute them over merchandise costs, add a preset profit, and crank out the prices. One weakness of this method is that the merchandise has to be sold, and in sufficient quantities to push you past the breakeven point. Another more glaring weakness is that full-cost pricing presupposes that your accounting system is able to capture all the costs and make accurate forecasts.

Since all pricing strategies are competitive, a major factor in your choice will be what the other guys are doing.

Consider setting prices above your competitor's prices if your	Yes	No	?
market is not sensitive to price changes			*some price sensitivity*
market consists mainly of growing commercial customers	X		
product is an integral part of an established system	X		
reputation for status, service, and other positive perceptions in the market increases your product's perceived value	X		
customers can easily build your price into their selling price	*yes?*		*not sure*
product is only a tiny percentage of your customers' total costs	X		

Consider setting your prices just below your competition if	Yes	No	?
your market is very sensitive to price changes	*somewhat*		
you're attempting to enter a new market		X	
your customers need to reorder parts or supplies		X	
your business is small enough that a lower price won't threaten your larger competitors and start a price war	X		
you have the option of economical production runs which decrease your unit cost			*n/a*
you have not reached full production capacity		X	

FIGURE 6.4 Price Setting Thoughts

Estimating demand

1. Which products/services do customers shop around for? _____

2. Which products/services are in greater demand even at higher prices? _____
   _____

3. Are certain products/services in greater demand at one time of the year than another? If so, which? And what is the duration of the demand? _____

4. Do your customers expect a certain price range? _____

5. What is the balance between price and quality in your market? _____
   _____

The competition

1. What are your competitor's pricing strategies? _____

2. Are your prices based on an average gross margin consistent with your competition's? _____
   _____

3. Is your policy to sell consistently at a higher price, lower price, or the same price as your competitors? Why? _____

4. How do competitors respond to your prices? _____
   _____

Pricing and market share

1. What is your present market share? _____

2. What are your market share goals? To increase share? Maintain share? _____
   _____

3. What effect will price changes have on your market share? _____

4. Is your production capacity consistent with your market share goals? _____
   _____

Strategy

1. Have you determined how pricing affects your sales/volume goals? _____
   _____

2. How can pricing help you gain new business? _____
   _____

3. Have you tested the impact of price strategies on your markets? _____

4. Are your strategies in line with broader economic trends? _____

Policies

1. How does the nature of your products/services affect their price? _____
   _____

2. How does your method of distribution affect price? _____

3. Do your promotional policies affect prices? _____

FIGURE 6.5 Pricing Checklist

Whatever you do, don't slap a price on your products and refuse to change it when conditions change.

The advantage is that full-cost pricing makes pricing simple. It is most helpful as a guideline, and can help narrow the price ranges set earlier.

- *Gross margin*. This can be figured either as a markup (adding a percentage of wholesale cost to your base cost) or as a markon (percent of the retail price represented by the gross margin).

  This method takes operating costs and market factors into account, but is only as good as your ability to meet projected sales levels. The big advantage is that gross-margin pricing helps set uniform price floors. You can then change prices to reflect market conditions, the market's sensitivity to prices, competition, and so on.

- *Flexible markups*. This is less rigid than full-costing, and is particularly helpful during periods of fluctuating prices. It demands that you have information about your market's sensitivity to price changes.

The main weakness of this approach is that it is all too easy to pursue sales at the expense of profit. While you don't want to hold on to inventory too long, you don't want to give it away either. This is a problem all merchants have to grapple with.

The best method of all is to combine the strengths of these four methods. Set firm price ranges for each product/service or product/service line, keep an eye open for competitive moves, and check constantly to ensure that your prices serve your profit and other marketing objectives. Whatever you do, don't slap a price on your products and refuse to change it when conditions change. Rigidity is as great a danger as being totally reactive to every market whim.

Try to ascertain factual answers to the questions in Figure 6.5 when you set pricing policies.

Summary for Chapter Six

- Pricing objectives are set, and a pricing policy that serves the sales, profit, and marketing goals of your company has been considered.

CHAPTER SEVEN

LOCATION AND SALES PRACTICES

The traditional 4 Ps of marketing are product, price, promotion, and place. Place includes location, distribution, and all intermediary channels between you and the end user. Location is straightforward. Where is your business located? If you have branch offices, where are they?

Distribution is a bit more complicated. You have to make a decision whether to sell directly to the consumer or go through a wholesaler or other intermediary, and then make decisions about those intermediaries (agents, retailers, or wholesalers). A graphic artist might choose to work directly with an author—no intermediary involved—or for a publisher, who is an intermediary between the graphic artist and the author. A sunglass manufacturer might choose to sell direct, or through a retail chain, an agent, or wholesalers, or use a new channel like the Internet. Each channel has its appeal. While a direct channel allows you more control it also involves you in the physical distribution of product, which may not be the best way to invest time and money. Many intermediaries are powerful sales engines, very knowledgeable about their markets, and well-staffed to serve them. Allying with them might be a shrewd move.

Some retailers, notably Wal-Mart, have added a high degree of sophistication to distribution. Wal-Mart's regional hubs, linked to their stores by the latest in electronic communications, make it possible to keep inventories lean and fresh. This gives Wal-Mart a price edge as well as an inventory edge. They can turn their merchandise rapidly (a function of lean inventories) and at the same time use their enormous purchasing power to drive down supplier prices.

Many intermediaries are powerful sales engines, very knowledgeable about their markets, and well-staffed to serve them.

QUESTION 20

How does your location affect you?

According to Small Business Administration studies, the most common reason to pick a new business site is "noticed vacancy." Since the three most important factors in retail business are "location, location, and location," it is no surprise that many small businesses never reach their potential.

If you are already in business, you still have to keep track of your trading area. Maybe you're considering a move to a new location, or building a branch office. New roads are constructed. Populations shift, zoning ordinances are altered, competitors come and go. If you can identify the advantages and disadvantages of your location, you can do something about them.

How do you evaluate the strengths and weaknesses of your location (actual or proposed)? While some businesses don't have to worry much about location, most do. If location is important to you, get answers to the following questions:

- *What is the traffic flow at the site?* Exposure to pedestrian and vehicle traffic will affect sales and advertising. See Figure 7.1 for some ideas.
- *What are the other stores or offices in the area?* Complementary businesses help. It's no accident that there are clusters of stores in almost every city. Automobile alleys, fast food restaurants, and department stores are three such clusters. Shopping malls are ideal for some businesses; others prefer stand-alone sites. Every major hospital is surrounded by health-industry related small businesses: doctors' offices, pharmacies, nursing homes and so forth.

> If you can identify the advantages and disadvantages of your location, you can do something about them.

You need two traffic counts, one for pedestrians and one for vehicular traffic. You should find out

❏ how many people pass by during your business hours;

❏ when they pass by;

❏ who these people are;

❏ where they are from;

❏ what their shopping plans might be;

❏ how many are logical prospects for your products or services;

❏ if there are seasonal or other predictable fluctuations;

❏ where they currently buy your kind of products or services.

These pieces of information help you to evaluate your site. Your advertising and other promotional programs also need this information.

FIGURE 7.1 Traffic Counts

By: __GL__   Date: __2/15/03__

1. How does the site affect your business? __Not too much—our business is generated by word of mouth and ads.__

2. How does the appearance of the building affect your business? __It's   OK—successful   and professional looking; not too plush.__

3. Does the store's or office's appearance complement your business's image? __It doesn't hurt.__

4. Do you (or can you) use the location to your best advantage? How? __Our office is easy to find.__

5. Should you move or consider moving? Why? __Not yet__

6. Is the neighborhood changing? If so, how? How will it affect your business? __Yes—businesses and the local economy are growing.__

7. Is the site high- or low-rent? __Moderate__

8. Is the rent competitive for the area? __Yes__

9. If your site is low-rent, how will you attract customers? _____

10. Is the location good from a competitive viewpoint? __It's OK—maybe we should think about moving downtown?__

11. Is the traffic sufficient for your sales objectives? __not applicable__

12. Will neighboring stores help draw customers? __not applicable__

13. Is parking adequate? Would paying for customer parking make sense? __Yes__

14. Can you develop additional traffic? How? __not applicable__

15. What disadvantages does the site have? How will you overcome them? __None__

16. Is this the best site available for your business? If no, why not? __It is adequate for now.__

FIGURE 7.2 Site Evaluation

MORE KMART WOES

Kmart's older stores feel out of date to today's shoppers. They don't appeal to the would-be upscale consumer.

Many of Kmart's locations present truck access problems. Wal-Mart's distribution model utilizes regional hubs to constantly dispatch trucks full of in-demand merchandise, thus securing economies of scale—keeping costs down with fresh merchandise always available. But trucks can't get to all Kmart stores in such timely ways. So the product selection suffers from location too.

Unless you have very good reasons to do otherwise, find out where businesses similar to yours tend to be located and join the trend. Trade associations, industry publications, and your own observations can help here.

Transitional areas pose a special opportunity and challenge. In many cities, for example, the downtown areas are coming back after years of blight. Ask the local realtors, chamber of commerce, bankers, city officials, and regional planners what's happening. They all will have good ideas and suggestions for you to evaluate and perhaps act on.

- *How's the parking?* Is the site easily accessible? Safe? Convenient? Unless you have a downtown location where parking is of no concern, this is a big question. It doesn't matter what the traffic count is if people can't find close, adequate, and safe parking.
- *What are the costs involved?* Rent = Space Costs + Advertising. A poor location will compel you to spend more on advertising, while a great location allows you to spend less. As examples, shopping center rents are high, but the traffic flow in a good one justifies the cost. A low rent, while appealing, will be offset by increased advertising costs. The totals may be the same.

> It doesn't matter what the traffic count is if people can't find close, adequate, and safe parking.

QUESTION 21

What are your sales practices?

Don't assume that your current method is the only way you can move your products or services.

Examining and improving selling methods is part of your marketing plan.

How are you currently selling your products? For example, a medical service might be sold solely by referral from a local hospital or by word of mouth—or through more assertive methods. Most stores rely on location, plus a minimum amount of advertising in local media.

You might be able to add sales by adding direct mail, using sales representatives, or direct, belly-to-belly selling. What changes might result in more sales? Are you cross-selling to your current customers, or merely taking orders?

What are your competitors' selling practices? If they are adding salespeople, or changing their advertising strategies, or moving to a new location, better take note. How do they get new customers and retain old ones?

"Shop" the competition, either in person or by using a consultant who will provide a detailed analysis of their sales methods. While you're at it, have your own business shopped. Close to 75 percent of lost customers complain of rude, discourteous, or poorly informed salespersons—and the irate customer complains to an average of 11 other people. That's powerful negative word-of-mouth.

> "Shop" the competition, either in person or by using a consultant who will provide a detailed analysis of their sales methods.

By: _GL_   Date: _2/15/03_

Competitor: _S, B & R_

Location: _Portsmouth_

Rate 1 (poor) to 5 (excellent)	Rating	Comments
1. Appearance and design of store	5	They've been around for a long time, and they are well-known. Also, they have a very good location.
2. Employees' characteristics		
A. Telephone manners	4	
B. Courtesy	4	
C. Helpfulness	4	
D. Appearance	5	
E. Product knowledge	4	
F. Ability to handle complaints	3	
G. Ability to cross-sell	4	
3. Availability of products	4	
4. Convenience of location	5	
5. Added services (delivery, etc.)	4	
6. Other (specify):		

FIGURE 7.3 Shopping Competition (Including Yourself)

By: ___GL___   Date: ___2/15/03___

Product or Service: ___Explanation of client's financial statements___

My Pricing Objectives	What Objective Will Accomplish	Time Frame for Reaching Objective
1. To charge an average of $200-$300 per month	A "door opener" for more business	Right now
2.		
3.		
4.		
5.		
6.		

FIGURE 7.4 Pricing Objectives

By: ___GL___   Date: ___2/15/03___

Product or Service: ___All accounting services___

My Pricing Objectives	What Objective Will Accomplish	Time Frame for Reaching Objective
1. Focus on the auto industry	Make us experts for that trade; we'll get referrals too	1 year
2. Develop local market	Save us time on the highway	Right now
3. Attend sales training program	Improve our skills	6 months
4.		
5.		
6.		

FIGURE 7.5 Sales Practice Objectives

AFTER SALES SERVICE ANECDOTE

One recent evening a telephone sales representative from Sears called my wife and asked, "Have you bought any major problems from us lately?"

After we finished laughing we agreed he probably had meant product or appliance, not problem. I have a Craftsman radial arm saw that I dote on, plus a gaggle of other power tools. We have a Kenmore dishwasher, refrigerator, and clothes dryer. None of these is on a service contract because I like to try to fix things if they stop working—a questionable economy but one that affords me considerable pleasure.

This wasn't the first time we had been offered a service contract. We've always said "no." We've filled in and returned forms saying no thanks, told sales clerks "no thanks," told other phone solicitors no thanks. Sears doesn't seem to listen. I've bought Craftsman tools because I know if they break I can easily replace them, sometimes at no cost. Besides, I think they make durable tools that are a good value for the money. We have purchased major appliances from Sears for the same reasons—they are durable and a good value for the money. If they break and I can't fix them, the Sears repairman comes and even if the appliance is nearly 30 years old (this actually happened), he can fix it, inexpensively.

What does this have to do with customer service? Everything. Consider: The salesman was poorly trained. Sears doesn't understand that we just aren't interested in buying service contracts. They tarnished their valuable asset—our perception that Sears products are durable, easily and economically repairable—by implying that we need a service contract because their products will need expensive repair. Why else would we need to buy insurance?

What follow-up do you have after the sale? Your best prospects are your current customers. If you don't provide adequate service after the sale, that customer will end up buying from your competition. Our ancient Maytag washing machine began to emit strange rumblings and squeals. My wife called the repairman who arrived with the requisite belts and fixed the machine the same day. That's great after-sale service.

If you never have repeat customers as part of your marketing strategy, fine. But for 99 percent of businesses, repeat sales are vitally important (and frequently overlooked in the scramble for new customers). Since you buy customers with your advertising and promotion efforts as well as your products and services, it makes sense to hang onto them as long as possible.

How should you follow up? Direct mail is excellent and can be low-cost. Phone calls are good. Maintain a service desk or a call-in number. Set a strong return policy favorable to the customer.

Follow-up differentiates your business from all the others. Satisfied customers talk. So do dissatisfied customers. Think of the effort Sears puts into its service department. Think of how a good auto dealer provides after-sales service, or how L.L. Bean and Nordstrom's handle customer returns.

Your best prospects are your current customers.

What kind of sales training do you provide? Salespeople aren't born knowing how to sell, and while you may be able to impart all the product knowledge they need, sales training is a highly specialized field.

If you don't provide sales training, why not? If it's on the grounds that sales training is something like advertising, an expense you'd rather not incur, you can count on being swamped by your competitors. You can find excellent sales training workshops through the Small Business Administration's SCORE and SBDC programs, at local colleges, or by asking your chamber of commerce. Sales training is as good an investment as you can make in your business's future. It has a fast payback, improves morale, and puts money in your pocket. What more could you ask for?

Figure 7.4 is a repeat of Figure 6.1. This is deliberate. As you examine and re-examine your pricing objectives you will also be thinking strategically: What are you trying to accomplish? Does it make sense given your resources and situation? How will your pricing policies affect your markets?

Summary for Chapter Seven
- Your location has been analyzed (see Figure 7.2).
- Sales practices—including training—have been examined, and your competitors "shopped" to ascertain their sales strengths and weaknesses (see Figure 7.3).

CHAPTER EIGHT

STRENGTHS AND WEAKNESSES

Your marketing strategy has to reflect the strengths and weaknesses of your business. This includes the competitive strengths and weaknesses noted in Chapter Four.

In a successful business, all important parts of running the business are covered adequately if not necessarily brilliantly. No major area can be left unattended. A management audit (see Figures 8.1 and 8.2) helps you gauge the quality of your management, spot areas where improvement is needed, and make sure that there are no glaring omissions to trip you up.

Your aim is to establish the right balance for your business. Your business is an assembly of systems, each of which has to work well for the whole business to be profitable. The audit helps make sure that your business has all its necessary parts, that they are all working together towards the same goals, and that the goals are suitable for the resources of your business.

Further, all parts should be of the right size. Letting one part outgrow the rest leads to an imbalanced allocation of resources. As you conduct your management audit, which should take only an hour or so to complete, keep balance in mind.

Any item that is checked "no" warrants your immediate attention because it flags a weakness in your business. While a "yes" answer affirms that the area in question is at least covered, there could still be room for improvement. You may want to go over Figure 7.1 again looking for "yes" areas that you can improve on. Remember: build on strengths, shore up weaknesses.

Figure 8.1 covers general internal operations. Section 1, Sales and Marketing, has the most direct bearing on your marketing plans.

Your aim is to establish the right balance for your business.

By: _GL_   Date: _2/19/03_

Based upon your analysis of the business, the operation is being run satisfactorily in the area of:

	Yes	No
I. Sales and Marketing		
A. Pricing		
Are prices in line with current industry practice?	x	
Is your pricing policy based on your cost structure?	x	
Have you conducted price sensitivity studies?		x
B. Market research		
Have you identified target markets?	x (some)	
Do you segment your markets?		x
Have you identified customer wants/needs?		x
Do you know how your markets perceive your products?		x
Has your business taken advantage of market potential?	x	
Has the competition been analyzed?	x	
C. Personal selling		
Do you know what your sales practices are?	x	
Does personal style influence your sales practices?	x	
D. Customer service		
Is customer service a priority?	x	
Do you solicit customer feedback?	x	
Is there a rational balance between serving your customer's needs and good business practice?	x (most of the time)	
E. Advertising and public relations		
Do you select media for measurable results?	x (not always)	
Is your advertising consistent?		x
Does your advertising budget make sense in terms of the level of business and its anticipated, planned growth?		x
F. Sales management		
Are salespersons and outside agents properly directed in their duties?	x	
Do you establish individual sales goals?	x	
Do you provide adequate sales support?		x
Are your salespersons trained?		x
G. Market planning		
Do you have a marketing budget?		x
Do you have a market plan?		x
Has your business taken advantage of market opportunities?		x

FIGURE 8.1 Management Audit

	Yes	No
II. Business Operations		
A. Purchasing		
Are reputable, competitive vendors used?	N/A	
Do you have a purchasing program?	N/A	
B. Inventory control		
Do you know your inventory turn?		
Is slow-moving stock managed?	N/A	
Have you established rational reordering policies?		
C. Scheduling		
Do goods and materials move through the business without tie-ups and problems?	x (usually)	
Do you know how long each job should take?	x	
D. Quality control		
Are inferior incoming materials returned to vendors?		
Are reject rates minimized?		
Do you have a "do it right the first time" policy?	x	
E. Business growth		
Has your business grown at least above the rate of inflation?	x	
Have you met your asset growth, sales, and profit goals?	*we didn't have goals— we need them!	
F. Site location		
Do you have the right business site?	x	
G. Insurance		
Do you have an annual insurance review?		x
Are the proper risks to your business (including yourself) covered?		x
Do you put your insurance package out to bid every year?		x
III. Financial		
A. Bookkeeping and accounting		
Are your books adequate?	x	
Are records easy to access?	x	
Can you get information when you need it?	x	
Do you have monthly P&Ls (income statements)?	x	
Do you have annual financial statements?	x	
B. Budgeting		
Do you use a cash flow budget?	x	
Do you use deviation analysis monthly?	x	
Are capital equipment purchases budgeted?	x	

FIGURE 8.1 Management Audit, continued

	Yes	No
C. Cost control		
Are cost items managed?	x	
Are high cost items treated separately?		
Is the budget used as the primary cost control tool?		x
D. Raising money		
Have you been successful in raising capital when it was needed?	x	
E. Credit and collection		
Do you use credit to judiciously increase revenues?		x
Do you know your credit and collection costs?		x
Is your current policy successful?		
Do you review credit and collection policies regularly?	x	
Do you have a receivables management policy?	x	
F. Dealing with banks		
Is your relationship with your lead banker open and friendly?	x	
Do you use more than one bank?	x	
G. Cost of money		
Do you compare the cost of money (interest, points) with your profit ratios?	x	
Are interest rates and loan conditions appropriate?	x	
H. Specific tools:		
Do you know and use:	x	
1) Break-even analysis?	x	
2) Cash flow projections and analysis?	x	
3) Monthly P&Ls (income statements)?	x	
4) Balance sheets?	x	
5) Ratio analysis?	x	
6) Industry operating ratios?	x	
7) Tax planning?	x	
IV. Personnel		
A. Hiring		
Has the right mix of people been hired?		x
Do you hire from a pool of qualified applicants?	x	
Do you maintain a file of qualified applicants?	x	
B. Training		
Are your employees suitably trained for their jobs?	x	
C. Motivating people		
Do your employees appear to enjoy what they are doing?	x (not all the time)	

FIGURE 8.1 Management Audit, continued

	Yes	No
D. Enforcing policies		
Does there seem to be logic and order to what goes on in the business?	x	
Are reviews and evaluations performed on schedule?		x
E. Communicating		
Are people informed and brought in on decisions?	x	
Do you create opportunities for employees to set their own goals?	x	
V. Administrative Management		
A. Record keeping		
Are records of past transactions and events easy to find?	x	
Are records retained for at least the minimum legal time period?	x	
Is access to personnel files limited?		x
B. Problem solving		
Are there few unresolved problems?	x	
C. Decision making		
Are you decisive?	x	
Is there a decision process (chain of command)?	x	
D. Government regulations		
Are you aware of local, state, and federal regulations that affect your business?	x	
E. Leadership		
Do you actually take charge of the business and its employees?	x	
F. Developing subordinates		
If you were to die or be suddenly disabled, is there a ready successor?	x	
G. Business law		
Do you have a working knowledge of applicable business law: contracts, agency, Uniform Commercial Code, etc.?	x	
Do you know how current contracts and other legal obligations affect your business?	x	
H. Dealing with professionals		
Do you have and use an accountant, attorney, business consultant?	x	
Do you use outside advisors?	x	

FIGURE 8.1 Management Audit, continued

However, if all of the other systems aren't in balance your plans won't work—so the more general operational review has to be taken very seriously.

The next form, Figure 8.2: Good Management Scorecard is a way for you to find out your own strengths. It will also help you identify those areas where you can improve your performance. If you have unbalanced

	Yes	No
I. We operate with a complete and up-to-date business plan which includes:		
A. One and three year projections		x
B. A capital budget		x
II. We operate with an annual marketing plan which includes:		
A. Precise sales and profit goals and timetables	x	
B. Strategies and tactics for the next three years		x
C. Budgets, forecasts, and benchmarks	x	
D. A tentative sales plan	x	
Our marketing plan also includes:		
E. The demographics of our target markets		x
F. A thoughtful definition of the markets we serve	x	
G. A definition of the needs/wants our products and services fill	x	
H. An analysis of the growth potential of our markets	x	
I. A competitive analysis		x
J. A definition of our "Unique Selling Proposition"		x
K. Projections for other products or services that could be developed	x	
L. Timetables for research and development		x
III. We use monthly budgets and statements which include:		
A. Thorough and up-to-date records	x	
B. Cash flow budget	x	
C. P&L (income) statement	x	
D. Balance sheet	x	
E. Deviation analysis	x	
F. Ratio analysis	x	
G. Standard cost comparisons		x
H. Cash reconciliation	x	
IV. We have developed an information base that allows us to:		
A. Keep track of new developments in the industry	x	
B. Obtain and study key trade information	x	
C. Understand what "state of the art" means in this business		x
D. Provide customers with the best available information pertaining to our products and services	x	
E. Keep all our employees adequately informed	x	

FIGURE 8.2 Good Management Scorecard

	Yes	No
V. I'm certain that the business is properly capitalized since I:		X
A. Base capitalization on worst-case planning		X
B. Have emergency funds (or access to them)		X
C. Have discussed this with our commercial banker		
VI. I understand the value of the business because I've made use of:		X
A. Professional appraisers		X
B. Present value methods to evaluate terms		X
C. Professional tax planning counsel	X	
D. Accurate, timely financial information		
VII. We strive to improve production, quality and operations by:		X
A. Keeping the plant in top condition	X	
B. Maintaining safe conditions	X	
C. Establishing high standards	X	
D. Standing behind our products and services	X	
E. Not tolerating shoddy performance	X	
F. Working for consistency	X	
G. Using our company's "look" as a statement to our markets		
VIII. Personnel decisions are based on humane, carefully considered policies which include:		X
A. Checklists to make sure objectives are clear		X
B. Communication, to make sure objectives are understood		X
C. Written job descriptions		X
D. Regular progress and performance evaluations	X	
E. Fair hiring practices	X	
F. Fair wage scales		
IX. As for my own personal/managerial skills, I work hard to:	X	
A. Develop my problem-solving abilities		X
B. Always stay calm		X
C. Be objective	X	
D. Avoid investments in my own ego	X	
E. Listen to my employees	X	
F. Plan changes in our course to minimize negative effects	X	
G. Make decisions promptly		X
H. Always get the facts behind problems	X	
I. Accept my own limitations	X	
J. Delegate tasks that can be done more efficiently by someone else	X	X
K. Analyze all available options	X	
L. Develop my reading/study habits	X	
M. Improve my skills	X	
N. Consider and evaluate risks		
O. Be positive with customers, employees, associates		

FIGURE 8.2 Good Management Scorecard, continued

QUESTIONS TO ANSWER

- Which products/services are most important for your customers?
- Which products/services are least important for your customers?
- What important proposals or bids have you won this year? Why did you win them?
- What important bids or proposals have you lost this year? Why did you lose them?
- What aspects of your advertising and public relations have been the most successful this past year?
- What aspects were the least successful?
- Which target markets or customer groups created the most sales for your business? Which created the most profits?
- Which target markets or customer groups created the fewest sales? The least profits?
- What additional goods or services will you need to remain competitive in the future?
- What did your business do best this year?
- What were your greatest triumphs?
- What were your greatest disappointments or failures?

skills, you may wish to balance them by taking a course, hiring the right skills, or delegating those areas where you are uncomfortable to someone already working with you.

Once more, "no" answers are red flags. "Yes" answers indicate acceptable levels, but may offer ideas for improved performance.

The next step is to relate your findings directly to your marketing plans. "No" answers to any item in Figure 8.1 or 8.2 present areas where you have a golden opportunity to improve your business's performance. A weakness identified is a problem half-resolved. Those "yes" answers that identify areas of particular strength should also be noted; they are strengths to build on.

> A weakness identified is a problem half-resolved.

Your search for strengths and weaknesses goes further. *External* opportunities or threats also have to be identified. You did this in a rough and ready way in Chapter One, Figure 1.4. Check your earlier list, and then fill out Figure 8.3. It may have the same items, but probably will not.

Figures 8.3, 8.4, 8.5, and 8.6 hark back to your initial SWOT analysis in Chapter One. If there have been no changes, beware!

QUESTION 22

What are your business's strengths?

Internal strengths are under your control. The strengths (and weaknesses) indicated in Figures 8.1, 8.2, and 8.3 can be augmented by your colleagues and employees. Your perception of what goes on may not be shared by

Factor	Opportunities	Threats
Current customers	*upgrade current customers*	

Prospect
  *motorcycle dealers, RV
  dealers, as well as other
  auto dealers*
	*deepens our market penetration;
	easier to sell as referral; very
	similar markets*	

Competition		
Technology		
Political climate		
Government and other regulatory bodies		
Legal		
Economic environment		

FIGURE 8.3 External Analysis: Opportunities and Threats Revisited

others. They may have a different feel for internal strengths and weaknesses than you do, and will almost certainly have different notions about the opportunities and threats posed by the external environments affecting your business. Get their input. This helps you widen your perceptions and helps your employees buy into the SWOT process and the changes that a SWOT analysis may lead to.

Strengths may be things like a great product, skilled personnel, super location, close relationship with an ad agency, or outstanding technology. You want to find as many of these as possible to help you more sharply define your marketing niche.

Opportunities are external, and include a number of factors you have little control over. For instance, your competition may be feeble, or your market expanding, or the local economy booming. These opportunities tend to be temporary: no economy booms forever, markets do have limits, and weak competition opens the doors for stronger competitors. Still, you want to be aware of and carefully monitor such opportunities so you can benefit from them.

Opportunities are external, and include a number of factors you have little control over.

QUESTION 23

What are your business's weaknesses?

Samples of internal weaknesses include weak, untrained, or underutilized personnel, lack of sales support materials, frequent stockouts, poor quality, and under-capitalization. While some weaknesses may have to be addressed from a company-wide point of view, some are essentially marketing problems. Do you have a marketing budget? If not, why not? Do you have sales training? Why not? Are sales support systems weak? Strengthen them.

Your awareness and understanding of external *threats* help you handle them. Maybe you face new, aggressive competition, or the local economy is taking a nosedive, or your market is evaporating due to a new technology. You have to know what these larger forces are to intelligently respond

By: _____   Date: _____

Our most important strengths and best opportunities are:

1. _customer service_
2. _financial management_
3. _bank relations_
4. _service quality_
5. _presence in auto-related market_

Our most dangerous weaknesses and threats are:

1. _capital_
2. _market planning_
3. _pricing (maybe!)_
4. _advertising and PR_
5. _____

FIGURE 8.4 Strengths and Weaknesses

#1 Weakness or threat	capitalization
Action	invest more
#2 Weakness or threat	strong competitors
Action	specialize, niche markets (auto, RV, motorcycle)
#3 Weakness or threat	market planning
Action	We're doing it now!
#4 Weakness or threat	advertising and PR
Action	contact several local agencies
#5 Weakness or threat	
Action	
#6 Weakness or threat	
Action	
#7 Weakness or threat	
Action	

FIGURE 8.5 Shore Up Weaknesses, Avoid Threats

#1 Strength or opportunity	customer service
Action	leverage—get more referrals; improve expertise in niche markets
#2 Strength or opportunity	financial management skills
Action	maintain; get deeper into auto/RV/motorcycle data
#3 Strength or opportunity	bank relations
Action	publicize; everyone has trouble getting financed these days
#4 Strength or opportunity	service quality
Action	? solicit testimonials
#5 Strength or opportunity	presence in auto and related markets
Action	run seminar; attend trade shows; publish "how-to" article in trade magazine
#6 Strength or opportunity	
Action	
#7 Strength or opportunity	
Action	

FIGURE 8.6 Build on Strengths, Seize Opportunities

to or preempt them. Maybe you can't control them, but you can control how your business reacts. If you predict external threats, you gain a sudden competitive advantage over the unprepared competitor. He or she gets swamped while you ride the wave.

List the strengths and weaknesses, both internal and external, that come to mind on Figure 8.4. Add those discovered in Figure 8.1, 8.2, and 8.3 above. Then go out and look for more. This is an open-ended process which will become second nature. As you identify the strengths and weaknesses, opportunities and threats, ask yourself:

- How can I take advantage of or build on this set of circumstances?
- If one or more are beyond my control, how will it affect my business?
- How long will these advantages and disadvantages last—and how can my business take advantage of these circumstances?

The next step in this process is to review Figure 8.4 and decide what to do about the most important weaknesses and threats. Since these represent significant problems, you want to focus your efforts on the most important.

Now turn to the more positive side of the coin. How can you take advantage of your strengths and opportunities? Once again, limit yourself to the most important—don't try to address all opportunities and strengths as if they were equally important.

> How can you take advantage of your strengths and opportunities?

Summary for Chapter Eight

- Two simple management audits have been conducted (see Figures 8.1 and 8.2) to discover internal strengths and weaknesses. In Figure 8.3 you looked at external opportunities and threats. After review, the most important strengths and weaknesses, opportunities and threats, were listed.
- These were then ranked in order of importance, and some of them singled out for immediate attention using Figures 8.5 and 8.6.
- Strengths and weaknesses help you or hinder you according to your awareness of them. If you are not reaching your sales and marketing goals, or if you think the goals should be higher, review this chapter.

CHAPTER NINE

ADVERTISING AND PROMOTION

With the possible exception of pricing, nothing causes more unnecessary confusion than advertising and promotion. If you have done your work so far, you will have a good feel for your markets—what they are looking for (their "what's in it for me?"), what the competition offers those markets, and what the members of the market read, watch, listen to, and attend. That massive amount of information makes it possible to tailor a message to your markets that will stir them to action.

First let's look at some definitions. There are six major methods of promoting a product or service.

1. *Advertising* is perhaps the most familiar form of promotion. We are bombarded by thousands of ads every day—in newspapers, on television and radio, on the Internet. One of the biggest problems with advertising is breaking through the clutter. We have all grown somewhat inured to advertising in self-defense.
2. *Public relations*, "the deliberate, planned, and sustained effort to establish and maintain mutual understanding between an organization and its publics" (the Institute of Public Relations' definition), is closely related to advertising. Although you don't buy space for public relations, it is not inexpensive.
3. *Direct mail promotions* (and the closely related e-mail promotions) target a population that is expected to have an interest in buying the product or service offered. Even the smallest companies can use this method, since all it basically calls for is a database or a mailing list.

One of the biggest problems with advertising is breaking through the clutter.

4. *Sales promotions* such as introductory offers, buy one get one free, coupons, and the infamous Ginzu knife's "But wait! Order now and you also get..." go beyond the usual advertising, public relations, direct mail, and similar promotions.

5. *Direct or personal selling* is a form of promotion best suited to expensive products (Rolex watches, luxury cruises). Here the person-to-person effort can explain the benefits of a product or service in whatever detail the customer desires.

6. *Trade shows* offer another means of promotion. While you may not generate many sales at a trade show, the people you meet and the exposure of your products or services to a wide range of other companies make these events an important part of your promotional mix.

The challenge all businesses face is how to put together a mix of promotions that is cost-effective, cuts through the clutter, and results in measurable sales increases. As in other aspects of business management, you will want to set goals, measure progress, and fine tune your promotional efforts as feedback indicates.

There are three myths to avoid.

1. *"You can rely on 'word-of-mouth' advertising."* This is usually an excuse to not invest in advertising rather than a good way to gain customers. Passive word-of-mouth is always ineffective. Happy customers tell an average of 0.7 other people if they have had a positive experience with you. Unhappy customers tell 11 to 20 other people. (Word-of-mouth advertising can be made to work, but it requires discipline and a programmatic effort: Ask customers for referrals. Make it easy for them to provide brochures, flyers, samples, or whatever it takes to make your case. Then follow up.)

2. *"Only highly creative and clever advertising works."* Not true. Clearly targeted and consistent advertising works. It does not have to be creative and clever. Some of the most effective promotions merely keep the name of a small business in the public's view: sponsoring a local team, running a consistent advertisement in the local paper, making sure to use the Yellow Pages. Nothing particularly creative or clever here, so it won't win prizes, but it works. The Super Bowl test is informative. With the exception of Apple's and Budweiser's advertisements, which are very memorable, what Super Bowl ads can you remember?

3. *"You can save money by doing your own advertising."* This is a bogus economy. Ineffective advertising is expensive. Advertising that does work, that informs your markets honestly, accurately and effectively, is worth its high initial costs. Professionals can put your message together faster and make it more effective than you can—especially since you can tell them who your customers are, and what, how,

> The challenge all businesses face is how to put together a mix of promotions that is cost-effective, cuts through the clutter, and results in measurable sales increases.

By: ___GL___   Date: ___2/21/03___

	Yes	No
Do you:		
Know where new business is coming from?	X	
Keep track of referrals and thank the sources?	X	
Track advertising and direct mail responses?	X	
Spend advertising dollars in proportion to your product mix?		X
Project a strong, consistent image in all materials, signage, stationery, and so forth?	X	
Have a professionally designed logo?		X
Sell benefits to customers in all promotional material?		X
Know what has worked, what has not worked, and why?	X	
Have a yearly advertising, public relations, and promotion plan?		X
Involve your entire staff in the promotional process?	X	
Advertise to your staff as well as to your markets?		X
Have strong relationships with media people and advertising professionals in your community?		X
Have a qualified in-house advertising/promotional person?		X
Assign one person to make sure your plan is implemented?		X
Have a professionally designed "facilities brochure" which explains what your business is?		X
Follow up promotional efforts with one-on-one selling (if appropriate)?	X	
Have professional window and point-of-purchase displays?		X
Have an appropriate Internet presence?	X	
Analyze your probable competition in connection with the direct and indirect sales promotional methods you use?		X

For any "no" or "?" answer, you have another reason to use a professional advertising/public relations/promotion agency.

FIGURE 9.1 Promotion Audit

when, and why they buy from you rather than from the competition. You've done the work, now let them do theirs.

Effective advertising and promotion is built on specific information, not on hunches or hopes. The reason to perform a promotion audit (see Figure 9.1) is so you can promote your business to its markets more effectively.

POSITIONING, PUBLICITY, AND PROMOTION

In *Ogilvy on Advertising*[1] David Ogilvy, founder of Ogilvy and Mather, wrote that of the 32 things his advertising company had learned, the most important was positioning. Positioning is a marketing method in which you determine what market niche your business should fill, and how it should promote its products or services in light of competitive and other forces.

Pick a niche in which you can become a presence. This can be as simple as locating your convenience store where there is little competition except major supermarkets, keeping hours to suit the convenience of your customers, and stocking the things they want at odd hours. Or if your local laws allow, become the only hairdresser who makes house calls. The idea is to differentiate your business from competing businesses, which means you must know what they are up to (hence the study of the competition) and who your customers are and what they want that other businesses aren't providing.

A market niche is much like a target market except (for most cases) a little more tightly defined in terms of how you can reach that market. Several specialty woodworkers in Boston advertise in the Boston Symphony Orchestra program and on educational television; they find this far more economical than buying space in a major daily or using network television. They zero in on their markets, using the proverbial rifle rather than a shotgun approach.

Targeted promotions to targeted markets is the safest way to stretch your promotional dollars and gain market share. By this point you should be able to decide what image and message you want to project: What will make your customers and prospects think of your business when they want to buy whatever it is you sell?

Since you know who your prospects are you can determine where your prospects are on the Promotional Pyramid. The notion behind the pyramid is that you can move people along one step at a time. If they don't know you're in business, let them know. If they know you are in business, what does it take to persuade them that you are going to be able to meet their needs? What will it take to get them to act? Do they understand what you want to sell them, or will you have to educate them first?

Locate the bulk of your customers and prospects on the Promotional Pyramid; then work with your advertising agency to move those customers and prospects along to the next level.

Acts

Convinced

Comprehends

Aware of your company

Unaware of your company

[1] Ogilvy, David. *Ogilvy on Advertising.* New York: Crown Publishers, 1983.

Your advertising and promotional efforts are adjuncts to more direct methods of selling, not substitutes.

Advertising and promotion are not substitutes for selling. Advertising is what you do when you can't have a salesperson work directly with the prospect. Advertisements can make prospects aware of you, make them

A successful promotional campaign requires answers to these six questions:

1. *Who?* Who are your customers and prospects? You have already segmented your markets, so you can describe who the promotion is aimed at. See Figure 4.1 in Chapter 4._____

   _____

2. *Why?* What are you trying to accomplish? Increase sales? Introduce a new product? Retain or increase market share? Create or maintain an image? See Question 25 in this chapter. _____

   _____

3. *When?* Timing in advertising is all-important. The best promotion will bomb if the timing is off. ____

   _____

4. *What?* What specific products or services are you trying to move? What is their unique selling proposition? _____

   _____

5. *Where?* What media would be best for your campaign?_____

   _____

6. *How?* Leave this one to your advertising agency. You have enough to do running your business. You have to review and approve the campaign. _____

   _____

The details—the "where" and "how"—are less important than getting your message out. Your ad agency will save you a lot of time here, help you make the right choices—and make the deadlines. Many good campaigns are sabotaged by well-intentioned business owners who know a lot about their business but little about advertising and promotion. Unfortunately, everyone thinks he or she is a good copywriter and art director. Nothing could be further from the truth.

FIGURE 9.2 Advertising Base

receptive to your products and services, even stir them to call or write for more information. But they can't replace ongoing sales efforts.

You have already done most of the groundwork for your advertising campaigns and other promotions. Effective creativity is based on thorough knowledge of products, target markets, and competitive conditions. Your advertising agency has to know what your objectives are, what your budget is, and when you plan to run your campaign.

Now fill in the answers in Figure 9.2.

Advertising and promotion have to be managed the same way you manage other parts of your business. You have to know what resources you can afford to commit to them (Question 24), and what you want to accomplish (Question 25), and form a coherent strategy that ties in with your broader business and marketing goals (Question 26).

Incomplete campaigns eat up money. You might as well burn the cash and save the time; you'd come out ahead. When setting up your promotional schedule, check with your advertising agency to make sure you have allotted sufficient time and money to complete your ad campaigns.

Advertising and promotion have to be managed the same way you manage other parts of your business.

PROMOTION = TIME + MONEY

TIME must be set aside for the following:

Task	Persons	Frequency Involved
Long- and short-term market planning	Key staff	Annually
Strategic planning for promotions	Key staff Agency	Semi-annually
Discussion of marketing and promotional goals and objectives	All staff	Quarterly
Discussion and evaluation of specific promotional activities and materials	All staff	Before and after each campaign
Implementation and scheduling	You Ad agency	Monthly or as necessary

Other important time-intensive promotional efforts include development and production of materials, all public relations activities, development and purchase of mailing lists, coordination of bulk mailings, writing and mailing individual letters and proposals, telephone, mail, and personal follow-up of promotional efforts.

Money must be set aside for

- public relations and general information materials, such as
  - printing
  - photography
  - sponsorship of events
  - open houses
  - mailings
  - community service advertising
  - donations
  - memberships (Rotary, chamber, service clubs)

- targeted product and service campaigns
  - copy writing and design fees
  - media placement costs
  - photography, typesetting, and graphic costs
  - printing
  - bulk mail (fulfillment)
  - mailing lists
  - studio and talent costs of radio/TV spot production
  - advertising fees other than copy and design

QUESTION 24

What is your advertising and promotion budget?

If you don't have an advertising and promotion budget, you don't have a rational marketing plan.

Advertising and promotion is a cost of doing business. Rigorously and ruthlessly suppress the urge to cut it at the first sign of sluggish sales. Build it in, like payments on plant or equipment or any other fixed cost, and be prepared to increase it. An advertising campaign is like a military campaign. Attaining your objectives calls for careful allocation and concentration of your resources so you can successfully implement your strategy.

You buy and maintain market share with advertising as well as with product, service, distribution, and other business efforts. When sales are off, increase advertising efforts. When sales are up, you may be able to ease off a little—run ads less often, for example. Reducing advertising costs when business starts to slow down will only accelerate a sales slump, not save your profitability.

How do you set an advertising budget? There are four common methods.

1. *Percent of sales.* You can get trade figures to show how others in your industry allocate their advertising dollars. Figure this on your anticipated or desired sales, and treat advertising and promotion as a fixed expense. If sales levels or goals increase, change the advertising budget. Do not cut advertising budgets in response to short-term sales slumps.

   This method is inflexible, and doesn't reflect the cost structures and marketing goals of your business. It does provide a good baseline. If you differ seriously from industry standards, have a good reason for that deviation and be prepared to justify that deviation to your banker.

2. *Flat dollar or "leftover" budget.* This is sometimes arrived at by adding all the other expenses and then allocating what's left to advertising. Another way is to take last year's advertising expenses and increase them a set percentage or amount.

   This leaves your advertising unbudgeted, campaigns incomplete, and your marketing efforts gutted. Flat dollar budgeting is far and away the most popular "budgeting" method for small-business owners, which should provide a competitive opening for you to take advantage of.

3. *Project-by-project or whim budgeting.* While this approach may enrich your advertising agency, it is effectively no budget at all. It lets you reduce advertising without noticing that you are doing so. It does have great flexibility, which is a strength if used in conjunction with a budget for ongoing advertising and promotional efforts.

4. *Flexible budgeting.* Set a lower limit, based on experience, industry standards, and sales goals. Then be prepared to increase it, on a project basis, to take advantage of opportunities or to turn a sales slump around.

   Smart small-business owners use two budgets to support their promotional campaigns. The first is a percentage of sales or flat-dollar budget for ongoing advertising and promotional expenses, while

When sales are off, increase advertising efforts.

These are goals some astute small-business owners have set for their advertising and promotional campaigns. This is intended as a nudge to your thinking, not as a comprehensive list of goals.

Do you want to

- penetrate specialized markets? Which ones? What are the measures of progress (unit sales, dollar sales, benchmarks)?

- sell more to present customers? How?

- specialize in terms of product or services? Which ones? Why?

- change your business's image? How? Why? To what?

- penetrate geographical markets more deeply? Which areas? How?

- create "top of mind" awareness? How?

- expand demographically? To whom? What market segments?

- increase sales of specific products or services? How?

- announce new product, new product mix, or new location?

- support community projects for public relations benefits?

Your answers to these questions decide how you want to be perceived, whom you plan to do business with, and what you want to sell.

FIGURE 9.3 Advertising/Promotion Goals

---

the other is a discretionary budget (project budget) with well-defined applications and dollar limits.

QUESTION 25

What are your promotional and advertising objectives?

If you reach your advertising objectives, you should be closer to attaining your marketing objectives. Advertising is tactical rather than strategic (see Figure 10.3: Current Strategy in Chapter Ten for a more detailed explanation). Your advertising goals serve your marketing goals, not vice versa.

QUESTION 26

How do you promote your business?

If you insist on doing your own publicity, promotion, and advertising, ask yourself once more: What business am I in? If it isn't self-promotion, then you'd do better to rely on outside advisors to help you set and implement your advertising and promotional policies. This is a specialized field, and too important an area for amateur efforts.

When you work with an advertising agent or public relations expert, the leading items on their agenda will be to determine

- what business you are in;
- what you want to accomplish with your advertising, publicity, or promotion;
- what you sell;
- whom you sell to;
- your sales and marketing goals;
- your budget; and
- your timetable for achieving your goals.

You can simplify and streamline much of the research and groundwork that effective advertising and promotion requires. Most of the work can and should be done by you. After all, it's your vision and experience and intuition that make your business special.

If these seem to be familiar questions, they are. Advertising and promotional campaigns begin with your current situation, rely on the budgetary guidelines to help you reach your goals, and absolutely demand thorough knowledge of what your business is and wants to become. And as you've seen by now, these are time-consuming questions to answer. Quick answers just aren't enough. You need facts, documentation, analysis, and more facts. The questions in Figure 9.6 at the end of this chapter will help focus your efforts.

An advertising plan (including promotional efforts) involves eight steps. Now that you know your advertising/promotional budget and your objectives, you can set down a preliminary plan.

1. _Identify long-term objectives._ These are objectives a year or more out. As always, make them as precise as you can: dollar or unit sales, time frames, persons responsible for attaining them, and some indication of the resources you can allocate to achieving them.
2. _Define short-term objectives and priorities._ What do you want to get done next month, next week, tomorrow?
3. _Assemble resources._ Have your in-house information available. A sketch of your options and priorities is helpful. Have your business plan near to hand.
4. _Select an advertising agency to guide you through the thickets of media selection and production scheduling._ See Figure 9.7.
5. _Schedule projects._ This is the heart of your advertising plan, and calls for a large calendar to help establish timelines. For each advertisement or project answer the following quetions:
   - Where will it run?
   - What is the "street date" when it will appear?

> You can simplify and streamline much of the research and groundwork that effective advertising and promotion requires.

- What size will it be?
- How much will it cost to prepare?
- What is the media cost?

Important considerations to keep in mind throughout the plan are timing, repetition (you get bored with the ad before your prospects and customers are aware that it's running), and reinforcement. Ads alone don't sell—but they create awareness and support your other selling efforts. You must spell out deadlines and assign responsibility to one individual (perhaps yourself) to make the most of your budget.

6. *Choose media.* See Figure 9.9 at the end of this chapter.

7. *Specs for ads.* Usually you leave this to your agency, but if you do it yourself, be sure to include the following:

   - Purpose of the ad: What do you want to accomplish?
   - Preferred approach: Hard sell? Soft sell? Humor? Fit the approach to your customers and your desired image.
   - Size and frequency of ad.
   - A creative budget.
   - Deadlines.

8. *Evaluate the results.* Unevaluated advertising might give you some short-run advantages, but if you can learn from your advertising and promotional experiences, your advertising can become more effective.

   You can test many elements of your advertising by following traditional methods. These work; they have been well proven.

   - Offer coupons.
   - Offer sales of certain items.
   - Split runs of your ad. (For example, run your ad in a national magazine only to certain geographic areas.)
   - Track inquiries. (For example, ask people to "write Department XYZ" for more information.)
   - Look for patterns of response (timing, numbers, percentages.)
   - Keep a scrapbook of your ads and other promotional efforts. Keep one for your competitors, too.
   - Ask your staff what they think of the ads.
   - Ask customers what they read and watch. See Figure 9.11: Ten-Second Media Quiz.

To illustrate the complexity of your advertising and promotion problem, look at the promotional methods in Figure 9.4. Your promotional mix will employ several of these, plus others that aren't listed.

One way to address the promotional mix is to use a form such as the following to make sure your advertising and promotions are targeted, not spread out mindlessly over the entire community. The three blank boxes

---

Important considerations to keep in mind throughout the plan are timing, repetition and reinforcement.

Promotion encompasses a wide range of activities. Some will be appropriate for your business and your markets; some will not.

Paid Advertising
- ❏ Radio
- ❏ Television
- ☒ Internet
- Print
  - ❏ Newspapers
  - ❏ Magazines
  - ❏ "Shoppers" (free or classified ad magazines)
  - ☒ Yellow pages
  - ❏ Local telephone directories
  - ❏ Special directories (regional, seasonal, chamber of commerce)
  - ❏ Trade or industry directories (e.g.: *Thomas' Register of Manufacturers*)
- ❏ Cooperative or "co-op" ad support from your vendors
- ❏ Transportation advertisements (subways, busses)
- ❏ Billboards

Direct Mail
- ❏ Letters
- ☒ Newsletters
- ❏ Sales or product/service announcements
- ☒ Flyers
- ❏ Postcards
- ❏ "Special customer" offers
- ❏ Brochures
- ❏ Direct response
- ☒ Internet newsletter   *Aim at information needs of auto dealers*
- ❏ Coupons
- ❏ Bill stuffers

Public Relations
- ❏ News releases
- ☒ Articles in magazines, journals, etc.   *We should do more of these!*
- ❏ Open houses
- ☒ Speaking engagements
- ❏ Interview shows
- ❏ Sponsorship of community events and activities
- ☒ Seminars
- ☒ Workshops
- ☒ Service club membership and participation
- ❏ Other club memberships

FIGURE 9.4 Promotion Smorgasbord

Telemarketing
- ❏ Inquiry handling
- ☒ Direct marketing by phone
- ❏ Service: customer complaints, follow-up, special offers

One-on-one selling
- ❏ Presentation materials   *We need this!*
- ☒ Personal letters
- ☒ Customized proposals
- ☒ Some telemarketing
- ❏ Sales personnel training   *We need this, too.*

Sales promotions
- ☒ Discounts   *1/2 hr. free consultation*
- ❏ Loss leaders
- ❏ Coupons
- ❏ "Buy one, get one free"

Specialty advertising
- ❏ Matchbooks, key chains, and other novelties
- ❏ Calendars   *We could use coffee mugs with our name*
- ❏ Date books   *and phone number on them.*

Facilities
- ❏ Site location and shared advertising
- ❏ Signage
- ❏ Window displays
- ❏ Point-of-purchase
- ❏ Fixtures and layout of store
- ❏ Lighting

Other types of promotion
- ❏ Flyers
- ❏ Posters
- ❏ Handouts
- ❏ Blimps and balloons
- ❏ Sandwich boards

Choosing the right promotional mix for your business calls for professional skills.
Check with your advertising and/or public relations agency.

FIGURE 9.4 Promotion Smorgasbord, continued

Type of Promotion	Audiences Targeted			Target Date	Estimated Costs
	Automobile dealers	RV & motorcycle	Heavy equipment		
Advertising: newsletter and/or magazine	X	X	X		
Advertising: radio and/or television					
Advertising: other					
Home page or other Internet presence	X				
Direct mail	X	X	X		
Newsletter	X	X	X		
Yellow pages	X	X	X		
Flyers and brochures	X	X	X		
Public relations: press releases					
Sponsorship	X	X	X		
Open house or other special event					
Specialty items (e.g., matchbooks, T-shirts)					
Seminars or workshops	X	X	X		
Telemarketing	X	X	X		
Other					

FIGURE 9.5 Promotional Summary

Ask and answer these questions:

1. Markets
    What is your market mix?
    What percentage of your business comes from:

individuals?	15%
small businesses?	75%
big businesses?	10%
local trade?	80%
regional trade?	20%
national or international trade?	

2. Products/services
    Are your products:

innovative?	x
specialized?	
diversified?	x maybe too diversified—a problem!
commodity?	
packaged?	
tailor-made or customized?	x

    (Answer "how" to each yes answer.)

3. Image
    Would you describe your business as:
    formal?
    informal?   x
    community focus?
    regional or national focus?   } We can't decide
    aggressive?
    relaxed or laid-back?   } 50/50
    sophisticated?
    "down-home"?
    specialized?
    generalist?

    Does that description fit the way you want to be perceived, as well as the way you see yourself now?
    Or do you want to change your company's image?   *We need to create one!*

4. Business strengths
    What special expertise, experience, and interests do you enjoy?
    longevity in the community?
    convenient location?
    outstanding service reputation?   x
    other: (specify)

FIGURE 9.6 Advertising/Promotional Questions

5. Competition
   How do you stack up against your competition:
   market share   *Low penetration*
   image

6. Customer base
   Do you sell:
   many products and services to a few loyal customers?   ×
   several products to a narrowly defined industry?
   single products to a diverse client base?   ×

   Do you have a database to tell you:
   product mix for each customer?   ×
   where their business came from? (referral, advertising, etc.) ×
   basic demographics of your markets?   *We should get one!*

FIGURE 9.6 Advertising/Promotional Questions, continued

Questions to ask when shopping for an advertising or public relations agency:

1. *What process does your agency use in analyzing client needs?*
   A successful program includes as much or more planning as execution. You want to be sure that the agency has the "mental horsepower" to see beyond the obvious and move your promotional programs beyond the limits of your own abilities.

2. *Once you've determined my needs, what is the process used to position my company?*
   The agency has to be your partner in developing a creative strategy for your business. What process do they use to develop your communications goals? Why?

3. *How do you measure how effective your strategies are?*
   Results can be measured in attitude changes, exposure, awareness, sales increases, specific information requested—and other ways. Make sure you are comfortable with their measurement plans, and that you understand why those are valid measurements. Be very leery of "You can't measure the results, but . . ." excuses. If it can't be measured, you can't afford it.

4. *How do you keep us informed about your activities?*
   You should get tear sheets, comprehensive and understandable billing, and full explanations of what is going on when you request it. The smoke-and-mirrors approach is fine for movies, but not for your investment.

5. *Who else have you worked with, especially similar to firms like mine? What success (and horror) stories do you have? Who may we contact?*
   Customers, both happy and unhappy, provide the least biased information about how well performance matched expectations.

6. *Describe a successful program for a business like ours. What were the goals of the program? What strategies and tactics did you use? How did you measure your success?*
   You want to separate fact from selling. Ask for names and numbers.

FIGURE 9.7 Selecting a Promotional Pro

7. *If the campaign is Public Relations (PR or unpaid advertising), what are your relationships with the media? Are you on a first-name basis with "influencers" in our field?*
Nothing is as helpful as a personal friend in high places. PR firms work to establish these relationships, and are (usually) proud of them.

8. *How do you approach creativity? How do you measure it? How do you involve clients in the creative process?*
The aim is to find out if they value creativity as a tool (good) or as an end in itself (bad). This is a judgment call you have to make—once again, smoke and mirrors are fine for entertainment, but not for your money.

9. *What important clients have you lost in the past year? Why did you lose them? May I speak with them?*
An agency that badmouths a former client will eventually badmouth you. Every agency loses clients to their competition; good agents know why and aren't ashamed or antagonistic about it.

10. *Most important of all: Who will be working on our account day-by-day?*
You want to have experienced talent working for you, not the newest hire. You can't afford to train beginners. Make sure the agency's top talent is working for you.

FIGURE 9.7 Selecting a Promotional Pro, continued

	Print Ad	**Two-Color Brochure**	**Coupon**	**Letter/Press Release**
Choose publication	1–7 days	Not applicable	Not applicable	1–3 days
Assign tasks/hire professionals	1–2 days	1–2 days	1–2 days	1 day
Write	1–4 days	1–7 days	1–2 days	1–3 days
Edit	1–2 days	1–3 days	1 day	1–2 days
Design	1–4 days	1–7 days	1–2 days	1–2 days*
Get estimates for printing/choose printer	Not applicable	1–3 days	1–2 days	1 day
Photography	2–7 days*	2–7 days*	Not applicable	2–7 days*
Illustration	2–7 days*	2–7 days*	Not applicable	Not applicable

FIGURE 9.8 Production Timelines

	Print Ad	Two-Color Brochure	Coupon	Letter/Press Release
Paste-up	2–4 days	2–7 days	1–2 days	1–2 days*
Printing/proofing	Not applicable	1–3 weeks	1–3 days	1–3 days
Total time	1–4 weeks	2–8 weeks	1–2 weeks	1–3 weeks

* If necessary

Production timelines for a well-designed Web page are very similar to those for a two-color brochure. They may be longer if your designer comes up with a strongly interactive Web site. See http://www.rcparker.com for an excellent example.

FIGURE 9.8 Production Timelines, continued

	Advantages	Disadvantages
Newspapers	• Your ad has size and shape, and can be as large as necessary to communicate as much of a story as you care to tell. • The distribution of your message can be limited to your geographic area. • Split-run tests are available to test your copy and your offer. • Free help is usually available to create and produce your ad. • Fast closings. The ad you decide to run today can be in your customer's hands two days from now.	• Clutter—your ad has to compete for attention against large ads run by supermarkets and department stores. • Poor photo reproduction limits creativity. • A price-oriented medium—most ads are for sales. • Short shelf life. The day after a newspaper appears, it's history. • Waste circulation. You're paying to send your message to a lot of people who will probably never be in the market to buy from you. • A highly visible medium. Your competitors can quickly react to your prices.
Magazines	• High reader involvement means more attention will be paid to your advertisement. • Less waste circulation. You can place your ads in magazines read primarily by buyers of your product or service. • Better quality paper permits better photo reproduction and full color ads. • The smaller page (generally 8½ by 11") permits even small ads to stand out.	• Long lead times (generally 90 days) mean you have to make plans a long time in advance. • Higher space costs plus higher creative costs.

FIGURE 9.9 Media Advantages and Disadvantages at a Glance

	Advantages	**Disadvantages**
Yellow pages	• Everyone uses the yellow pages. • Ads are reasonably inexpensive. • You can easily track responses.	• All of your competitors are listed, so you run the ad as a defensive measure. • Ads are not very creative, since they follow certain formats.
Radio	• A universal medium—enjoyed at home, at work, and while driving. Most people listen to the radio at one time or another during the day. • Permits you to target your advertising dollars to the market most likely to respond to your offer. • Permits you to create a personality for your business using only sounds and voices. • Free creative help is usually available. • Rates can generally be negotiated. • Least inflated medium. During the past ten years, radio rates have gone up less than other media.	• Because radio listeners are spread over many stations, to totally saturate your market you have to advertise simultaneously on many stations. • Listeners cannot refer back to your ads to go over important points. • Ads are an interruption to the entertainment. Because of this, radio ads must be repeated to break through the listener's "tune-out" factor. • Radio is a background medium. Most listeners are doing something else while listening, which means your ad has to work hard to be listened to and understood. • Advertising costs are based on ratings which are approximations based on diaries kept in a relatively small fraction of a region's homes.
Television	• Permits you to reach great numbers of people on a national or regional level. • Independent stations and cable offer new opportunities to pinpoint local audiences. • Very much an image-building medium.	• Ads on network affiliates are concentrated in local news broadcasts and on station breaks. • Creative and production costs can quickly mount up. • Preferred items are often sold out far in advance. • Most ads are ten or thirty seconds long, which limits the amount of information you can communicate.
Internet	• Reaches a target audience. • Highly interactive. • Can provide enormous amounts of information at a very low cost. • Very flexible: you can change your pages quickly as conditions, products, and prices change. • Links to other sites can spread your reach.	• Reaches only the computer-literate. • Lots of Internet clutter that may make your site hard to find. • A new (albeit fast-growing) medium.

FIGURE 9.9 Media Advantages and Disadvantages at a Glance, continued

	Advantages	Disadvantages
Direct mail	• Your advertising message is targeted to those most likely to buy your product or service. • Your message can be as long as necessary to fully tell your story. • You have total control over all elements of creation and production. • A "silent" medium. Your message is hidden from your competitors until it's too late for them to react.	• Long lead times required for creative printing and mailing. • Requires coordinating the services of many people: artists, photographers, printers, etc. • Each year over 20% of the population moves, meaning you must work hard to keep your mailing list up to date. • Likewise, a certain percentage of the names on a purchased mailing list is likely to be no longer useful.
Telemarketing	• You can easily answer questions about your product/service. • It's easy to prospect and find the right person to talk to. • Cost effective compared to direct sales. • Highly measurable results. • You can get a lot of information if your script is properly structured.	• Lots of businesses use telemarketing. • Professionals should draft the script and perform the telemarketing in order for it to be effective. • Can be extremely expensive. • Most appropriate for high-ticket retail items or professional services.
Specialty advertising (balloons, sandwich boards, key charms, etc.)	• Can be attention grabbers if they are done well. • Can give top-of-mind awareness. • Gets your name in front of people.	• Difficult to target your market. • Can be an inappropriate medium for some businesses. • It's difficult to find items that are appropriate for certain businesses.
Word of mouth	• Low cost. • Natural extension of personality of business. • Keeps customer needs in clear view. • This is an important adjunct to your other marketing efforts.	• Word of mouth is very dependent on levels of quality and customer service. • Must be managed carefully. Ask for referrals. Provide collateral advertising material to your customers. • Sometimes used in lieu of any other promotional efforts, which is dangerous.

FIGURE 9.9 Media Advantages and Disadvantages at a Glance, continued

Please list the newspapers you read regularly.

	Daily	**Weekly**
1. First choice	_____	_____
2. Second choice	_____	_____
3. Third choice	_____	_____

This really doesn't apply to us.

Please list the radio stations you listen to regularly.

1. First choice _____

2. Second choice _____

3. Third choice _____

4. Fourth choice _____

5. Fifth choice _____

Have you recently seen or heard our advertising?
Where? _____

Thank you for your help!
Your Logo

FIGURE 9.10 Ten-Second Media Quiz

on the first line are for specific target or niche markets. See the examples at the end of the chapter.

Summary for Chapter Nine

- You completed a promotion audit (see Figure 9.1) to determine where you need professional advertising help.
- You looked at what goes into planning a promotional campaign (see Figures 9.2 and 9.3) and different ways of promoting your business (Figures 9.4 and 9.5). You set objectives and reviewed your advertising budget.
- Figure 9.7 will help you evaluate ad agencies and choose the one most likely to help you reach your advertising and promotion objectives. Figures 9.5, 9.6, 9.8, and 9.9 will help you set an agenda with your ad agency.
- Work with your ad agency to develop an advertising action plan. Set a timetable for the objectives you want to reach, decide what actions are important and when those actions will be taken to implement these objectives, and how much money will be needed at specific times to achieve your objectives.

CHAPTER TEN

STRATEGIC MARKETING

"It is not enough to be industrious; so are the ants. What are you industrious about?"

—Henry David Thoreau

All marketing decisions are strategic. In Chapter One you went through a SWOT analysis to be able to build on your strong points and shore up the weaker ones. That's a strategy in itself, an active strategy that aggressively strives to take control of the business's future. Making a decision to market strategically follows from this initial decision.

How might this play out in the real world of competition and unexpected events? Ron Michaels, a marketing expert from Tucson, Arizona, offers two excellent examples: Michael's Marketing Maxims.

1. *Minimize opportunities for customer dissatisfaction.* Customers hate to be surprised and disappointed. Think of McDonald's motto "Quality, Service, Cleanliness." Their food may not be epicurean, but their bathrooms are so clean and the level of service so high and dependable that McDonald's owns the family fast-food business. Ever travel with children and not stop at McDonald's? They have minimized opportunities for customer dissatisfaction. You know what you are going to get—and you get it.

2. *Marketing wars are never won. They are always lost.* The importance of careful and consistent attention to the customer base cannot be overstated. When one business competes with another for the market's custom, the one who makes fewest mistakes will be the survivor. This isn't a defensive stance; it's a highly active process that

> The importance of careful and consistent attention to the customer base cannot be overstated.

continuously looks for ways to improve, improve, improve. Nothing fancy, just old-fashioned hard work.

Strategic marketing takes account of the competitive nature of business and keeps your efforts focused. All of the preceding chapters have implicitly taken a strategic bent. Now make your own strategy explicit.

Why consciously choose a marketing strategy? Your marketing efforts are goal-directed, and you want to be sure that the goals you are aiming at are the goals you wish to reach. Strategic planning makes sure that you do the right things. Your marketing plan helps you do those things right.

QUESTION 27

What marketing problems have you discovered so far?

> Your marketing efforts are goal-directed, and you want to be sure that the goals you are aiming at are the goals you wish to reach.

All businesses have problems. The strengths of your competition, your business's competitive weaknesses, technological changes, shifting public tastes—the list can go on and on.

Review Figures 1.6, 3.2, 3.5, 5.3, 5.4, 5.5, and all of Chapter Eight, especially Figure 8.3.

Ask yourself (and your staff and other interested persons) the following:

- What problems are you currently working on?
- What problems are you avoiding?
- What are you going to do about them?
- Who is responsible for solving these problems—and when? With what resources?
- Why haven't you reached your sales and/or marketing goals in the past?
- What might keep you from reaching your current sales goals?

QUESTION 28

How do you plan to solve these problems?

List several possible solutions to each major problem. Don't just pick the first solution that occurs to you. It might not be the best solution. The trick is to define the problem as factually as possible, then look for a number of possible causes. Facts and analysis will prevent you from solving the symptom rather than the disease.

Then ask yourself how your strategies will affect or be affected by these problems.

If problems have to be resolved, assign responsibility for solving each problem to one person. Make sure to allow enough authority and sufficient resources to that person (you or another). Maybe the solution will involve brainstorming or other techniques—the important thing is to first recognize the problem, then carefully define and analyze it before taking action.

By: ___GL_____   Date: _____2/24/03_____

1. What is the problem? Cite standard and deviation from standard if available.

   _We lack a single focus._____

   _____

2. Possible causes:

   _We've always taken all business that comes our way, and we haven't established a____

   _niche for ourselves._____

3. Interim solution:

   _Define short-term market goal: go after auto market._____

   _Do a profitability study to determine where time gets billed and whose time is wasted.___

FIGURE 10.1 Problem Solving Worksheet

QUESTION 29

Are the goals stated in Chapter One still valid? If not, what are your new goals?

Return to Figures 1.3 and 1.5.

Preliminary goal-setting was a starting point, not the final decision. Revise your sales and marketing goals in light of the analysis of the preceding chapters. Maybe the strategies that make the best sense for your business call for a revision of your goals.

If you do change some of your goals, what are the new ones? Collect them on Figure 10.2. Be as specific as you can. For example:

For next year

- increase sales of Product A 15 percent by December;
- lower reject rate 5 percent in the next quarter;
- open branch office in St. Paul in six months, with sales goals and budgets established by Harvey and approved by Maude due on my desk no later than September 15th.

And so forth. Goals have to be clear, measurable, and most important of all, easy to communicate. Your marketing strategies and plan are built to accomplish these goals—and people have to know what the goals are.

> Goals have to be clear, measurable, and most important of all, easy to communicate.

Personal goals include nonfinancial goals as well as financial goals. Limit the goals to the most important.

Most Important Personal Goals

- Improve health and increase level of energy
- Change the mix of work I'm currently doing
- Make more time to enjoy life
- Make more money
-

Business Goals

	Next Year	Three Years
Quantitative Goals		
• Sales ($)	$320	$500
• Sales (unit)		
• Profit ($)	$48	$75
• Profit (% sales)		
• Market share	15%	25%
• Company net worth ($)		
• Number of employees	5	8
Qualitative Goals		
• Market position	small business experts	more niche oriented
• Kind of business	accounting	more business consulting
• Target markets	auto businesses	auto related businesses
• Business culture or style	same	even more professional!
• Other (specify):	improve use of time	

Potential Conflicts Between Personal and Business Goals

We need to work out a marketing plan so our business goals reflect our personal goals. We'll need to add personnel if we are to grow.

Comments

FIGURE 10.2 Personal and Business Goal Summary

Fuzzy goals such as "increase sales" or "cut the reject rate" or "get that dratted branch going" are seriously deficient, don't provide the timetables or assign responsibilities, and as a result are not effective.

How do you plan to achieve these goals?

That's what your marketing plan is all about. Each goal calls for a series of actions. The strategies in Figure 10.4 set broad marketing objectives; the more specific goals in Figure 10.2 delimit the tactical boundaries. You won't attain your goals all at once, but rather in stages.

If you have chosen your strategies wisely, and made sure that reaching the goals of Figure 10.2 leads to attaining the strategic objectives, the steps should be clear. As with any tactical plan, you have to know what the goal

STRATEGIES AND TACTICS

All strategic elements must be defined in terms of needs, attitudes, and unmet desires in the market. These will include known needs that can be accurately determined by investigations and hypothetical needs that must be nourished to become a market need.

Tactics are	Strategies are
• concrete	• conceptual
• specific	• general
• individual	• complex
• linear	• organic
• sequential	• interactive and systemic

Strategic planning must define goals that are qualitative in nature. These qualitative goals include

- *Positioning.* What is the position of your organization in its target markets and among your competitors? How is it viewed by the market?
- *Segmentation.* What are the demographics and qualitative characteristics (attitudes and tastes) of your defined target markets?
- *Cultural.* What is the culture of your business?
- *Stylistic.* What is the style of your business?
- *Differentiation.* In what ways does your business and its product/service structure differ from all other organizations offering similar products and services?
- *Functional.* What purpose does the organization and its product/service structure fulfill beyond its own parochial needs?

Quantitative elements to be defined include price strategy, market share, growth rate, cost characteristics, sales and profit goals, production and distribution goals, and logistics.

is, when it is to be reached, what resources you have to attain that goal, and what the possible barriers are. Some of these details will be spelled out in the sales plan later in this chapter. Others will be treated in the Marketing Plan itself.

Selecting a marketing strategy is a four-step process.

1. Examine past and current marketing strategies. Have yours been "business as usual," "get whatever pieces of business we can," or "follow-the-leader"? These are the three common and ineffective strategies. Few small-business owners plan to run their businesses these ways, but inattention and habit make these choices inevitable.

You can't change strategies overnight. They are built into the culture of your business. Your goals and methods of achieving those goals (including business practices and relationships of people within the business) are inextricably mixed up with your strategic choices. The strategies and culture evolve together slowly; they change slowly too.

Your strategies should reflect your attitudes and personality. Strategies can be active or reactive, aggressive or defensive, risk-taking or risk-averse. If your own style is relaxed and risk-averse, an aggressive, high-risk strategy probably won't work. If you enjoy risk and being ahead of the crowd, then a defensive, reactive strategy will drive you up the wall. That doesn't mean you can't adopt a conflicting strategy for a short while—but if you adopt one counter to your feelings, be aware of the potential conflict.

Strategies can be active or passive, aggressive or defensive, goal-oriented or opportunistic. These three sets of pairs help you define your current strategies; apply them to each of the following areas and ask yourself which adjective applies out of each pair.

> Your strategies should reflect your attitudes and personality.

Your Current Strategy	Aggressive or Defensive?	Active or Passive?	Goal-Oriented or Opportunistic?
Marketing *CHANGE!*	defensive	passive	opportunistic
(Management)	defensive	passive	opportunistic
Financial	defensive	passive	opportunistic
Production	——	——	——
Operations	——	active	——

FIGURE 10.3 Current Strategy

Promotion encompasses a wide range of activities. Some will be appropriate for your business and your markets; some will not.

Paid Advertising
- ❏ Radio
- ❏ Television
- ❏ Internet
- Print
  - ❏ Newspapers
  - ❏ Magazines
  - ❏ "Shoppers" (free or classified ad magazines)
  - ❏ Yellow pages
  - ❏ Local telephone directories
  - ❏ Special directories (regional, seasonal, chamber of commerce)
  - ❏ Trade or industry directories (e.g.: *Thomas' Register of Manufacturers*)
- ❏ Cooperative or "co-op" ad support from your vendors
- ❏ Transportation advertisements (subways, busses)
- ❏ Billboards

Direct Mail
- ❏ Letters
- ❏ Newsletters
- ❏ Sales or product/service announcements
- ❏ Flyers
- ❏ Postcards
- ❏ "Special customer" offers
- ❏ Brochures
- ❏ Direct response
- ❏ Internet newsletter
- ❏ Coupons
- ❏ Bill stuffers

Public Relations
- ❏ News releases
- ❏ Articles in magazines, journals, etc.
- ❏ Open houses
- ❏ Speaking engagements
- ❏ Interview shows
- ❏ Sponsorship of community events and activities
- ❏ Seminars
- ❏ Workshops
- ❏ Service club membership and participation
- ❏ Other club memberships

FIGURE 10.4 Promotion Smorgasbord

Telemarketing
- ❏ Inquiry handling
- ❏ Direct marketing by phone
- ❏ Service: customer complaints, follow-up, special offers

One-on-one selling
- ❏ Presentation materials
- ❏ Personal letters
- ❏ Customized proposals
- ❏ Some telemarketing
- ❏ Sales personnel training

Sales promotions
- ❏ Discounts
- ❏ Loss leaders
- ❏ Coupons
- ❏ "Buy one, get one free"

Specialty advertising
- ❏ Matchbooks, key chains, and other novelties
- ❏ Calendars
- ❏ Date books

Facilities
- ❏ Site location and shared advertising
- ❏ Signage
- ❏ Window displays
- ❏ Point-of-purchase
- ❏ Fixtures and layout of store
- ❏ Lighting

Other types of promotion
- ❏ Flyers
- ❏ Posters
- ❏ Handouts
- ❏ Blimps and balloons
- ❏ Sandwich boards

Choosing the right promotional mix for your business calls for professional skills.
Check with your advertising and/or public relations agency.

FIGURE 10.4 Promotion Smorgasbord, continued

There is nothing normative about these pairs. No one is "better" than another though some are more useful for your business at one time than another.

2. Summarize personal and business objectives. Include your personal goals in your marketing plans. If you want to retire in 5 years, fine. Plan for it. If you want to work until you drop, fine. Plan for it. If you want your business to remain small enough so you can bring your dog to work, great. It can be done. Just don't set up your business to thwart yourself. If you want to see how big a business you can build, go ahead. Build the business. But not unless it makes sense to you, personally.

In Figure 1.3 you set down preliminary personal goals. Review them now. In Figure 1.5, you listed preliminary business goals. Review them also. If your personal priorities aren't in line with your business priorities, change your business priorities. You have better things to do with your life than warp it for the benefit of your business. Review Figure 10.2. Figure 10.5 should include all changes and revisions of your goals to date; it will be the basis of your marketing plan.

3. Now return to Figure 10.4. Examine each of these strategies and ask yourself if, given your resources and competitive situation, it would help you reach your goals. You will probably want to use more than one strategy, or modify one or more to better fit your business.

4. Choose the simplest strategies for your business. To be effective, strategies have to be communicated. Fancy strategies look great on paper, but if they present opportunities for misunderstanding, you can count on their being misunderstood. The simplest strategies are the best strategies.

Now make your final strategic choices.

- Test them for consistency with each other. You don't want to pursue contradictory strategies.
- Test them for feasibility. If they require more resources than you can muster, they won't work.
- Test them for coherence: Do they fit your business? Do they tend towards unifying the focus of your marketing efforts? Do they form an understandable, easily communicated grand strategy?
- Finally, make sure they are acceptable to your employees. If you can't generate company-wide support, the strategy will fail. This is where complicated strategies break down. If you can't communicate the strategies clearly, you have a problem. (This is a blessing in disguise. In competitive markets, your competition will look at your strategy and try to improve on it by making it a bit fancier here, a bit more complicated there. They can't resist. Let them be complex. You stay simple, and win the marketplace.)

To be effective, strategies have to be communicated.

Most Important Personal Goals

- Improve health and energy levels
- Build retirement portfolio to permit semi-retirement in 5 yrs.
- More personal time; balance with family
- Income: $80,000 after tax; plus profit from practice
-

Business Goals

	Next Year	Three Years
Quantitative goals		
• Sales ($)	$320	$500
• Sales (unit)		
• Profit ($)	$48	$75
• Profit (% sales)	15%	15%
• Market share auto, etc.	10%	30%
• Company net worth ($)	n/a	n/a
• Number of employees	5	8

Qualitative goals

- Market position   leader in selective niche markets
- Kind of business   profitable specializing MAS/consulting to selected markets
- Target markets   auto, RV, motorcycle, heavy equipment
- Business culture or style   professional
- Other (specify):

Potential conflicts between personal and business goals

   Time! How to manage time more efficiently, delegate better—

Comments

   Return to this in three months.

FIGURE 10.5 Personal and Business Goal Summary

This checklist presents a range of small business strategic options proven in hundreds of applications.

Past	Current	Future	Strategy	Probable Consequences, Risks
			Sample Marketing Strategies	
1.			Rationalize distribution. Cut back to most efficient network; look at volume, geography, type.	*Increase profit margins, lower inventories, some costs go down; may need new investment; moderate risk.*
2.			Develop the market. Create demand for a brand new product.	*Very high marketing costs, may increase receivables, impacts profit and loss statement, hinders cash flow; large expense budget; high risk—but high reward if successful.*
3.			Penetrate the market. Increase market share: lower price, broaden product line mix, add service and sales personnel, increase advertising.	*Increases marketing and sales expenses, need for working capital, and need for capital investment if capacity grows. Reduces short-term earnings; high risk.*
4.			Promote new products to present market. Develop, broaden, or replace products in product line, sell to present market.	*Lower unit costs; increase inventory, sales volume, profit and cash flow; some capital investment needed, increased development, design, and manufacturing costs; moderate to high risk.*
5.			Seek new markets, same products. Expand existing markets by geography (abroad) or type for existing products.	*Increase sales volume and profit margins as unit costs drop and as new market grows; higher short-term selling costs; modest capital investment, increased working capital; high risk.*
6.			Develop new products for new markets. Invest in developing, manufacturing, and marketing products unrelated to product line for new markets.	*Will increase sales volume, costs, profits (if successful); will have same problems as a new business if products unrelated to current line; will need more working capital, may need new capital investment; increase in sales and marketing costs; high risk.*

FIGURE 10.6 Checklist for Strategic Planning

Past	Current	Future	Strategy	Probable Consequences, Risks
			Sample Marketing Strategies	
7.			Rationalize market. Prune back to most profitable segments, higher volume segments; concentrate marketing focus.	*Reduce sales volume, increase profit margins, lower working capital needs, increase cash flow as percent of sales, decrease receivables; willingness to accept lower sales totals; moderate risk.*
8.			Maintain products and market share. Business continues as before; same products, same markets.	*Increase at industry growth rate with stable, short-term profit margins; decrease working capital and increase cash throw off overtime; may lower unit costs; investment in strategies to hold position; low risk.*
9.			Cut costs. Reduce costs uniformly through management edicts.	*Increase profit margins, achieve lowest possible return of all efficiency strategies; needs excellent implementation to apply intelligently; moderate risks due to arbitrary nature of cutbacks—may have invidious consequences.*
10.			Abandon unit. Sell or liquidate unit because it doesn't fit in with company—or because it is worth more to someone else.	*Improve cash flow from sale of assets, create possible morale problem in rest of organization; low risk.*
			Sample Financial Strategies	
11.			Rationalize product line. Narrow profit line to most profitable items.	*Reduce sales volume, improve working capital, profitability, may lead to underutilizing assets in short term; hard to give up old winners; low to moderate risk.*
12.			Pure survival. Hunker down to meet most adverse conditions by eliminating or paring down some aspects of the business.	*Reduce sales volume, considerably reduce costs, improve ROI short term, improve cash flow temporarily; courage needed, moderate risk due to possible loss of market share, some danger from creditors and other trade sources.*

FIGURE 10.6 Checklist for Strategic Planning, continued

Past	Current	Future	Strategy	Probable Consequences, Risks
			Sample Financial Strategies	
13.			Pause in action. Slow down or establish a one-year moratorium on new capital investment; normal maintenance of business.	*No effect on sales short term, may disrupt growth plans, weaken business over long term, decrease sales and earnings if pause is too lengthy; courage and large measure of steadfastness; low risk.*
			Sample Production Strategies	
14.			Improve technology. Improve operating efficiency through technological improvements in physical plant, equipment, or processes.	*Decrease variable costs and increase fixed costs—an overall reduction can considerably increase profits, affects sales volume slightly; low to high capital investment; low to moderate risk depending on the extent to which the particular technology is proven.*
			Sample Operating Strategies	
15.			Improve methods and functions. Invest in new ways of doing existing tasks by adding new 'soft' technologies: e.g., new patterns of work flow, CAD/CAM, production planning, inventory control, etc., to improve effectiveness and/or efficiency.	*Improve operating performance, improve functional rather than product costs; expense investment; creative thinking needed; low to moderate risk.*

FIGURE 10.6 Checklist for Strategic Planning, continued

Summary for Chapter Ten

- Marketing problems (and problems that might affect your marketing plans) were listed and addressed in Figure 10.1.
- Personal and business goals appear twice. Figure 10.2 is based on the earlier goals and objectives, as well as preliminary strategic thoughts. Figure 10.5 is the final result of Chapters One through Ten.
- Strategies for your marketing plan are indicated on Figure 10.4; the goals they are to help you attain are listed on Figure 10.5.

CHAPTER ELEVEN

THE MARKETING PLAN

Now you can assemble your marketing plan and give definitive answers to the three critical marketing questions: *What are your target markets? What products or services do they want from you? How can you best position your products and services?*

This chapter is one of review and revision leading to action. You have all of the parts to assemble the plan. You now want to make sure that the information fits together, is up to date, and has been thought through in the context of the current economy and competitive environment. Your plan is a tool for your use, and its value will be proven in its effective use. You implement your plan through the sales and promotional tactics it establishes. Your strategy sets the scope and direction of the actions; your sales and promotional tactics implement that strategy.

Your overriding marketing objective is to find people to buy enough of your products and services, for enough money, and often enough to ensure a solid profit margin. Your marketing plan helps keep your business focused on the steps necessary to reach or exceed your goals.

Your market plan should not be long. If it becomes much longer than 20 pages, it won't be used. Individual elements that back it up may be lengthy, however. An advertising/promotional plan, for example, may run much longer. Sales plans for individual products, product lines, or services can become immensely detailed.

The market plan must be succinct. It summarizes the analyses and strategies of the preceding nine chapters—so in one sense, you've already written it. Writing out your formal marketing plan gives you another chance to review your ideas and goals. If you haven't involved your staff in the planning process, this is a good time to get their ideas.

Your marketing plan helps keep your business focused on the steps necessary to reach or exceed your goals.

These are the four Ps of marketing. Make sure the aspects of each variable pertaining to your business complement one another.

Product/service

New, modified, new application
Position on life cycle
    Cash cow?
    Rising star?
    Dog?
    Problem child?
Benefits to purchaser
Perceived value
Will products/services be bundled or sold individually?
What is the product mix?

Price

To end user
To distributors and to trade
    (What margins do you allow distributors and trade?)
Image
Market penetration
Market's sensitivity to price changes
Premium, skim, meet market rates, penetrate?

Place

Will you sell direct or through agents, wholesalers, or other intermediaries?
Location
Signs
Direct mail
Direct sales
Telemarketing

Promotions

What mix of media will you use?
Advertising (including yellow pages, classified ads)
Internet
Public relations
Trade shows
Packaging
Special promotions (sales, spotlights, etc.)
Direct mail
Personal or direct selling
Sales force training
Marketing support
Image: point-of-purchase, layout, lighting, stocking
Personal letters
Circulars, brochures, flyers

FIGURE 11.1 The Four Strategic Marketing Variables

The key section of your marketing plan (see Figure 11.2) is Section 7: How to achieve your goals. You have four strategic variables to play with: product/service, price, place, and promotion. Each of these can be subdivided further (see Figure 11.1) and tailored to meeting the wants of your target markets.

There is no mechanical method of grinding out how to reach your goals. Your judgment and experience have to find expression here. The most common reason that strategies fail is that the fundamentals of implementing the game plan are done poorly or not at all. It doesn't matter how good your strategy is if it isn't properly executed.

The strategic variables must be considered in light of your present and prospective target markets. Your marketing plans focus on meeting the needs and wants of these markets.

A thorough consideration of the preceding "Four Ps of Marketing" is part of your review. Another part is to review your strategic plan from Chapter One. In particular, ask yourself:

- Does the mission statement reflect my personal goals?
- Are the business description and mission statement still accurate? If you think they should be modified, return to Figures 1.1: Business Definition Worksheet and 1.2: Mission Statement Worksheet. Fill them out again to reflect your newest insights.
- Review Figures 1.3: Internal Analysis, 1.4: External Analysis, and Figure 1.5: SWOT Summary. Do they need to be modified? If so, redo them.
- If the actions proposed in Figures 1.6: Building on Strengths and Opportunities and 1.7: Shore Up Weaknesses, Avoid Threats need to be revised, revise them.
- Should the long-term goals in Figure 1.8: Long-Term Goals be modified? If yes, revise them.
- Should the short-term objectives in Figure 1.9: Turning Goals into Objectives be revised? If yes, revise them.

Take these final reviews seriously. When you first worked through the "What business am I in?" exercises in Chapter One you set off on a path of discovery that will ordinarily compel you to change your mind about the directions and actions for your business. Now that you have worked through the first nine chapters, this is where you pull all of that effort back into a simple, clear strategy—that is, your marketing plan.

That's it. These assembled forms *are* your marketing plan!

Your marketing plan is not designed for outside review. Keep it in a three-ring binder (the forms fit nicely and are easily updated). Share it with your employees. Investors and bankers may also ask to see it, but most likely will be so pleased with the results that they won't want to peer into the details of your plan.

Your marketing plan defines the strategic directions for your business's marketing. The sales plan connects those grand strategies with your

> The most common reason that strategies fail is that the fundamentals of implementing the game plan are done poorly or not at all.

1. Mission statement
   (What you want your business, main markets, and products/services to be. See Figure 1.2, p. 5.)

2. Marketing objectives for next year and the next three years
   (These are the broad marketing objectives of Figures 2.5: Preliminary Marketing, Sales, and Profit Goals and 10.2: Personal and Business Goal Summary.)

3. Sales and profit goals for the next one and three years
   (See Figure 2.5: Preliminary Marketing, Sales, and Profit Goals and Figure 10.2: Personal and Business Goal Summary.)

4. Products/services
   (Brief description by product/service lines, including proposed changes and any recent changes that would affect marketing goals. See Figure 2.2: Product/Service and Market List.)

5. Target markets
   (List and briefly describe. See Figure 4.1: Who Are Your Customers?, 4.3: Basic Market Segmentation Criteria, and 4.7: Customer/Prospect Summary.)

6. Market potential
   (What size are the markets and what potential sales, profit, or other advantages does each have? See Figure 4.7: Customer/Prospect Summary.)

7. How to achieve your goals
   • Overall strategy
     (See Figure 10.6: Checklist for Strategic Planning.)
   • Competitive strategies
     (See Figure 5.7: Competitive Objectives.)
   • Promotion strategies
     (See Figure 9.5: Promotional Summary.)
   • Pricing, Place, Sales Practices
     (Brief statement of pricing strategy from Figure 6.4: Price Setting Thoughts, 6.5: Pricing Checklist, plus brief statements about location, hours, and selling practices from Chapter Six if important or changed from normal patterns.)
   • Marketing and advertising budgets
     (See Figure 2.8: Preliminary Marketing Budget Estimates and 9.5: Promotional Summary.)

8. Potential problems
   (Brief description, plus proposed solutions, from Figure 2.6: Problems.)

9. Implementation and measurement of timetables and benchmarks
   (See Figures 11.3: Marketing Action Plan and 11.4: Marketing Action Timetable.)

10. Review and evaluation schedule
    (Short schedule of important review dates.)

Appendix: Include supporting documents such as letters of intent and purchase agreements, if you think documentation is needed.

FIGURE 11.2 Suggested Outline of Marketing Plan

markets. Use Figure 11.3: Marketing Action Plan and Figure 11.4: Marketing Action Timetable to organize actions and assign responsibility for their achievement. The goals come from Figures 10.2 and 10.5.

Keep the following three major guidelines in mind:

1. *Establish objective, measurable goals with deadlines.* Broad, fuzzily defined sales goals are useless.
2. *Assign one person to oversee the action steps.* Shared responsibility means nobody is responsible.
3. *Discuss the action steps, timetables, and resources with the person responsible for attaining the objectives.* If possible, involve everyone who works on the objective; this helps assure their cooperation. If your employees know clearly what you are trying to achieve, why it is important to attain that goal in time and within the resources allotted, and how progress will be measured, they will come up with ways to reach that goal.

There are six steps to the marketing action plan.

1. State the goal.
2. Assign a target date for achieving the overall objective.
3. Assign responsibility to a single person.
4. Define the action steps. Achieving the objective requires that certain action steps be taken, in a logical sequence. The more definitive the action steps, the better—since they can be more easily monitored.
5. For each action step, assign a target date. You may also want to assign responsibility for finishing the step to another person; delegation may be the only way to attain these mediate goals. Include the resources needed for each action step, and keep track of them. (Budgets are needed here—but that's another matter.)
6. Track the results, for progress and for future use.

In Figure 11.3 you put together a *tactical* plan. Achieving the broad marketing objectives is like winning a war, while reaching these mediate goals is more akin to winning individual skirmishes and battles. The tactics—the short-term activities which must be marshaled together to reach the strategic objectives—are highly detailed, but governed by the broad strategic guidelines established beforehand. Tactics only make sense in the context of strategy. Otherwise they are just random, undirected actions.

You may wish to break this process down even further, and fill out one of these forms for each goal and each major action step involved. For example, if your goal is to increase net profits from product A by $10,000 by the end of the next quarter, you might find that you have a considerable number of action steps to take: hiring and training a new salesperson; preparing marketing support, advertising, and promotional materials; issuing a new guarantee; repackaging and repositioning the product or service; and opening a new target market—all the while making sure that it doesn't affect other lines.

> Achieving the broad marketing objectives is like winning a war, while reaching these mediate goals is more akin to winning individual skirmishes and battles.

By: _____GL_____   Date: __2/27/03__

Action Steps	Target Date	Person Responsible	Results
Identify 100 prospects	ASAP 3/03	G & B	
Call on prospects in reverse order of desirability—3 each wk.	9/03	G & B	
Make proposals to 10	11/03	G & B	
Close 3	12/03	G & B	
Develop home page; link to Portsmouth, NH home page	ASAP! 3/02	G & B	

FIGURE 11.3 Marketing Action Plan

> Your job as owner is to set the strategic goals and, with the persons involved, the tactical objectives.

Once you have arrived at the action steps and their tentative due dates, timing becomes more and more important. One way to handle the timing problem is to work backwards from the target dates. When do you have to start an action step? What steps along the way are critical to reaching the target dates? The more of these intermediate dates you can establish the better; they provide benchmarks to help keep the process of attaining the goals (and hence the strategic objectives) on schedule.

Use your judgment in choosing which steps to pin down to the tight scheduling of Figure 11.4: Marketing Action Timetable. You want to strike a balance between no controls and too much control.

Don't overdo this. Too much detail is stifling. Your job as owner is to set the strategic goals and, with the persons involved, the tactical objectives. Any finer detail is best left to the people involved. If they know what you expect and when, they'll do their best to meet those benchmarks and deadlines. Think of it this way: Would you rather have control in your job over how to achieve desired results (within limits of company policy) or would you prefer to have the job dumbed down with infinitely detailed to-do lists?

By: _____ GL _____   Date: ___ 2/27/03 _____

Action step: ___ Identify prospects _____   Target date: ____ 4/03 _____

Completed: _____   Not completed but due: __ 4/7/03 _____

List:

Sub-step	Completion Criterion (Benchmark)	Dates of Completion
1. yellow pages	3/15/03	3/12/03
2. D & B	3/22/03	3/13/03
3. Drive around	4/1/03	4/7/03
4. Clip ads from local papers	ongoing	ongoing
5. Internet	3/03	ongoing
6.		

FIGURE 11.4 Marketing Action Timetable

It's the same with your employees. Once again: State the goals. Give timely feedback on how well progress is being made towards those goals by breaking them into short-term objectives with firm deadlines. Make sure that the right resources are in place to achieve those objectives.

Summary for Chapter Eleven

- Figures 11.3 and 11.4 provide you with an implementation and control system for your marketing plan.
- If you assign product line (or service line) responsibility to an employee or colleague, work through these figures with him or her. The more people involved in setting the due dates and completion criteria the better. Their ideas on implementation can make a great contribution.

- A sales plan is simply a compilation of Figures 11.3 and 11.4 for each product and/or service. Since you work out the detailed steps one by one with the overall marketing plan strategies in mind, reaching these more limited goals will help you attain the marketing objectives.
- The reviews and evaluations help keep the plan on time and on target—and will help you improve your skills.
- The marketing plan makes sure that you do the right things. The sales plan is tactical; it helps you do things right. You need both.

CHAPTER TWELVE

MARKETING AND THE INTERNET

The Internet is a wonderful source of new marketing tools, methods, and ideas, but be aware that it is an addition to, not a substitute for, traditional marketing methods. The extraordinary hype surrounding the Internet has led some business owners to overinvest in e-marketing to the detriment of their core business. Some businesses benefit from the Internet. Some do not. Most can use it for market research, including checking up on the competition and performing market research. It is increasingly useful as a promotional tool. Most cities have a Web page that informs visitors about restaurants, stores, entertainment, and other businesses, much like a Yellow Pages in electronic format. As an example, check out <www.sea coastnh.com>, which covers the New Hampshire seacoast.

How might you proceed? Slowly and carefully. Start by asking yourself why you want to use the Internet in your marketing efforts and what marketing objectives you hope to achieve (including what resources in time, money, and equipment you are willing to invest). Then take some time to look at Web sites that are already up and running.

If after this initial research you believe that you can benefit from an Internet presence, the process is straightforward. You will have to secure a domain name (which is your Internet location), create a Web site, publicize the site's address, and be prepared to keep the site fresh, up to date, and interesting. Today's customers want speed (a slow Web site bogged down by too many graphics is a turn-off), convenience, personalization, and participation as well as information about your products and services.

How do you want to use the Web in your marketing efforts? The primary purpose of marketing is to acquire, enhance, and retain customers. This

> Start by asking yourself why you want to use the Internet in your marketing efforts and what marketing objectives you hope to achieve.

E-MAIL MARKETING

Don't overlook e-mail as a marketing tool. It is cheap, easy, effective, and everywhere. You can use it to communicate one to one. You can use or develop e-mail lists (listservs) to communicate with many people at once. Or you can use chat groups, discussion groups, or newsgroups to communicate with lots of people. Just be prepared—again—to respond quickly.

Consider the following e-mail marketing suggestions:

- Use e-mail to spread word of your Web site.
- Use Frequently Asked Questions (FAQs) to answer the most common questions about your business, products, or services. These can run 24 hours a day with no effort on your part.
- Make it easy to e-mail you, subscribe to your newsletter or other mail, and unsubscribe as well.
- Capture e-mail addresses. You can offer a premium, free information, updates, or even a newsletter or special report to entice people onto your e-mail list. How about a free sample?
- Post in relevant newsgroups, discussions, and other public spaces on the Internet. Urge people to sign up their friends and acquaintances who would be interested in your wares.

basic customer relations management lends itself to the Web. For example, I buy books from Amazon.com. They maintain a file on what I buy and send me notices of books (and other items) I might find interesting. This service upgrades me from a once-in-a-long time buyer to a relatively frequent purchaser. Their site keeps me involved by soliciting my opinions about books I purchase or have read; I can also read reviews by my peers. Amazon has an excellent fulfillment system that allows me to get a book overnight or opt for lower cost but slower delivery. Amazon.com does it right and has earned a huge market. They also enjoy a sky-high customer retention rate of around 60 percent.

You might want to sell products and services on the Internet, communicate with your markets, enter into a dialogue with your customers, expand your markets beyond a local presence, or just promote your business. Check out Dell Computer's site. They have managed to perfect their "build to order" business model. It's fast, easy, and effective. It is low cost due to their low inventories, and it's profitable. Their cash conversion cycle is a stunning eight days.

Who are your customers? How are their priorities changing? Some may be migrating to wireless application protocol (WAP) as more powerful handheld devices hit the market. What kind of relationship do you want to establish with them? Target marketing still rules. Are your products and services tailored to their demands? What can you offer them that makes dealing with you a pleasure?

What can you offer them that makes dealing with you a pleasure?

What marketing objectives do you hope to achieve? As with any marketing action, you need to have a budget and a timetable as well as metrics to mark your progress (or lack of progress). In the earlier part of this book you established your objectives and near-term goals. If you included Internet marketing objectives, great. If not, stop and decide what your Internet objectives are before going forward. Make sure to include the ongoing costs of updating your Web site. The costs can be significant. A stale Web site loses business. Due to the nature of the Internet a bad experience gets a lot of exposure via e-mail, chat rooms, and so on. How will you fulfill orders? Are you staffed to respond quickly? Internet buyers tend to be an impatient lot. (The profile of people who buy on the Internet is interesting. They tend to be young and technically proficient, or older with high incomes. This has obvious implications for any marketer.)

Check out competitive Web sites. Do your competitors (direct and indirect) have Web sites? What are they like? As with any competitive analysis, you aren't looking to copy what they do but rather to learn from them. Some of their ideas may be good, some not so good. You may find ways to improve on what they are doing—and in any case, you need to know what they are up to.

Choose your domain name. You have to choose and register your Web site's domain, which is its location on the Internet. If possible, make it close to the name of your business. Checking out the availability of a name is simple: there are services such as Network Solutions that will do this for you. Once you find an available name of your choice, you can register it through these services. (A Google.com search for "register domain name" turns up literally hundreds of registration and hosting service companies.)

As with any marketing action, you need to have a budget and a timetable as well as metrics to mark your progress (or lack of progress).

SOME GOOD WEB SITES

These are a few of my favorite business Web sites. They are quick, full of relevant information, interactive, and always up to date. Some are for small businesses, some for large—on the Internet, size is neither an advantage nor a disadvantage.

<www.llbean.com>   <www.travelocity.com>

<www.amazon.com>   <www.fromages.com>

<www.dearborn.com>   <www.in-n-out.com>

<www.dell.com>   <www.mahalos.com>

<www.nytimes.com>   <www.westmarine.com>

<www.fruitactivewear.com> <www.popswine.com>

Your name may have been taken already, in which case a little ingenuity is called for. FinestKind Seafoods in York, Maine, found that their name had already been taken. Since their Internet objective is to sell and ship lobsters, they settled on <www.finestkindlobster.com> as their domain name. Pay them a visit if you want fresh lobster.

Create your Web site. The key question to answer here is whether to hire a professional or do it yourself. There are certainly some price savings to be had by doing it yourself, but if your time is valuable or if you aren't adept at html (the computer language that runs your Web site) the savings may be illusory. Remember: the Internet is unforgiving. If your site is slow, dull, uninformative, or otherwise flawed the costs will far outweigh the money saved by doing it yourself, just as with any other form of promotion. Web sites that don't work are expensive. Web sites that do what you want them to are cost effective.

My recommendation is to hire a pro—after you have done some homework to lower the number of billable hours. Here is a checklist of items you can do yourself.

> Web sites that do what you want them to are cost effective.

- Choose the domain name and register it.
- Select a business-friendly Internet Service Provider (ISP). AOL and MSN are great for personal use, but clumsy and restrictive for business applications. A business which uses either is labeled beginner by the Internet cognoscenti.
- Make sure that both Netscape and Microsoft Internet Explorer are compatible with your site. It's easier to make sure before you begin than to rework the site after it is up and running. It's less embarrassing, too.
- List all the contact information you want to appear on your site: company name, address, phone and fax numbers, e-mail if you are prepared to respond to it, and pictures and brief bios of key personnel, customers, and suppliers.
- Have your logo and logotype available in electronic format.
- You may want to add product, price, and purchasing information, and company and industry news to your site—or perhaps add them later. In any case, make sure you have the capability of fulfilling orders if you plan to sell online.
- Decide how many pages you want to begin with. A well-done single page is better than a sloppy multiple-page Web site.
- Determine your budget. A good Web site isn't necessarily expensive, but there will be some unavoidable costs. Make sure you set aside enough money to complete the task. And remember to include the costs of updating and refreshing your site.
- You may wish to experiment with site construction. If you have AOL or MSN, they provide guided instructions on site construction at a very low cost. A personal Web site (you can put those pictures of

yourself holding big fish on your own page!) can give you a good feel for the complexity involved in creating an effective site.

- Make a list of the Web sites you wish to be connected to. Your Web professional can grapple with embedded e-mail links and metatags (the linking and search-capable mechanics). While it isn't difficult, he or she will have a better idea of which search engines (such as Google, Alta Vista, and Yahoo) will be best for your business.
- Check with other business owners whose sites you admire to identify Web professionals.
- Now interview those consultants who met your criteria.

When you hire someone to construct your Web site make sure it is clearly stated in the contract that he or she is performing work for hire, and that you (or your business) owns the site. Otherwise you may find yourself facing unexpected problems down the road.

When discussing your site with your consultant, stress the importance of simplicity; "keep it simple, stupid" (KISS), an old cliché, is always good advice. As time goes on you will most likely want to improve the site by adding graphics, fresh and timely content, and additional services and products. Again, a good working relationship with the consultant will pay off. What is the best "shopping cart" for your site? What is the best way to navigate from one page to another? How can you keep track of who is visiting your site? What should you do about privacy concerns? Will you or should you use cookies? Will on-site registration help you build a visitor list? What about accepting credit card orders? What kind of pictures will you use? Do you want to run banners (ads that can lower your costs but which might irritate your customers), or use pop-ups or other advertising material? This is a relatively new field and some of the protocols are still in flux. These kinds of questions should be familiar to your consultant. You rely on your lawyer's and accountant's expertise in fields you don't have time to master. Do the same for your Internet consultant—you have better uses for your time.

Now if you still want to do it yourself, fine and dandy. Go for it. There are a number of helpful books on using the Internet for marketing and e-business. IDG Publishing's _Internet Marketing for Dummies_ by Frank Catalano and Bud Smith is a good place to start. _Roger C. Parker's Guide to Web Content and Design_ by Roger Parker (Hungry Minds) provides a good introduction to the Internet's marketing capabilities. In addition, pay a visit to <www.internet.com>, which will link you to a deep reservoir of Internet marketing expertise. However, I warn you that this is a very complex and time-consuming do-it-yourself project.

Test run your Web site. Have some friends and a few customers review it before rolling it out. Up to this point the decisions on design and content have been in your hands. A reality check by outside eyes can be most illuminating.

> When discussing your site with your consultant, stress the importance of simplicity.

If you have a college or university nearby ask the communications or marketing professor specializing in Internet design to have students review your site. This is a particularly helpful demographic: young, computer savvy, somewhat jaded—and probably opinionated as well. All of you will benefit. If suggestions are offered, take them seriously. The odds are good that you will want to make a few corrections and tweaks before rolling out the Web site.

Publicize the Web site in every possible way. Your polished site is now up and running, but unless you let people know about it you will only get random visitors. Make sure your universal resource locator (or URL, your site's address) appears on your stationery, business cards, brochures, bills, space advertisements, direct mail, and other print media. Put it on a billboard so rush hour drivers get to see it. Put it on T-shirts. The more you can publicize your site to your intended markets the better the payoff will be. This will take time, especially if your domain name is obscure. The links and metatags built into your Web site will stir up some traffic. Since this is a shifting source (links come and go in popularity, and new buzzwords appear to siphon off search engine time) it will be part of the ongoing maintenance of your site. And so will the constant publicizing of your URL.

Maintain and refresh your Web site. It is surprising how finicky the Internet public has become. The biggest complaints are speed (how long does it take for the site to load?), complexity of navigation (ever get trapped in a Web site?), and stale content. Speed and complexity develop incrementally as you add new features and new content. While you are blinded by familiarity your visitors are not. This is another call for either a consultant or a dedicated in-house expert to make sure the speed, complexity, and content are handled professionally.

> The more you can publicize your site to your intended markets the better the payoff will be.

SECURITY

Computer security is an obvious concern for any business that operates online. While there are many ways to protect your computers against viruses (commercial programs such as McAfee, Dr. Solomon's and Symantec are well proven), protection against a dedicated hacker involves another level of protection. The Library of Congress Web site <www.loc.gov/global/internet/security> is well worth a visit. They have FAQs, links to many sites and discussion groups, and alerts, bulletins, and other sources of information. This is too important to leave to chance or learn by trial and error. Get professional help.

Summary for Chapter Twelve

The Internet can open new markets for you, assist in two-way communications with your markets, provide a new sales channel, and more. But enter it carefully. The technical complexities are daunting. The expense (unless you carefully budget) can get out of hand. Build slowly and carefully, check your progress against the metrics you have chosen (number of hits on your Web site, click-throughs, actual dollar sales, comments from customers and prospects) and be prepared to continuously upgrade and refresh your Internet presence. The Internet is no magic bullet—but it is a very powerful tool if properly used.

SUMMARY OF QUESTIONS AND MARKETING PLAN OUTLINE

Summary of Major Questions

Chapter 1 The Quick Strategic Marketing Plan

Question 1   What business are you in?

Chapter 2 Marketing Overview

Question 2   What do you sell?

Question 3   Who are your target markets?

*Question 4   What are your marketing goals for next year?
                Your sales and profit goals?*

Question 5   What might keep you from achieving these goals?

Question 6   What is your marketing budget?

Chapter 3 Products and Services

Question 7   What are the benefits of your products and services?

*Question 8   What is the Unique Selling Proposition (USP) of
                your products and services?*

*Question 9   What product or service is the best contributor to
                your Overhead and Profits (O&P)? Your worst?*

Chapter 4 Customers and Prospects

Question 10   Who are your current customers?

Question 11   What are their buying habits?

Question 12   Why do they buy your goods and services?

Question 13   Who are your best customers and prospects?

Question 14   What is your market share?

*   a. Is your market share growing, shrinking, or
                   stable?*

*   b. Is the market itself growing, shrinking, or stable?
                   Is it changing in other ways?*

Chapter 5   Competitive Analysis

Question 15   *Who are your competitors?*

Question 16   *What do your competitors do better than you?*

Question 17   *What do you do better than your competitors?*

Question 18   *What is your competitive position?*

Chapter 6   Price Setting

Question 19   *How do you establish prices?*

Chapter 7   Location and Sales Practices

Question 20   *How does your location affect you?*

Question 21   *What are your sales practices?*

Chapter 8   Strengths and Weaknesses

Question 22   *What are your business's strengths?*

Question 23   *What are your business's weaknesses?*

Chapter 9   Advertising and Promotion

Question 24   *What is your advertising and promotion budget?*

Question 25   *What are your promotional and advertising objectives?*

Question 26   *How do you promote your business?*

Chapter 10   Strategic Marketing

Question 27   *What marketing problems have you discovered so far?*

Question 28   *How do you plan to solve these problems?*

Question 29   *Are the goals stated in Chapter One still valid? If not, what are your new goals?*

Question 30   *How do you plan to achieve these goals?*

Outline of a Marketing Plan

1. *Mission statement*
   (What you want your business, main markets, and products/services to be. See Figure 1.2: Mission Statement Worksheet.)

2. *Marketing objectives for next year and the next three years*
   (These are the broad marketing objectives of Figures 2.5: Preliminary Marketing, Sales, and Profit Goals and 10.2: Personal and Business Goal Summary.)

3. *Sales and profit goals for the next one and three years*
   (See Figure 2.5: Preliminary Marketing, Sales, and Profit Goals and Figure 10.2: Personal and Business Goal Summary.)

4. *Products/services*
   (Brief description by product/service lines, including proposed changes and any recent changes that would affect marketing goals. See Figure 2.2: Product/Service and Market List.)

5. *Target markets*
   (List and briefly describe. See Figure 4.1: Who Are Your Customers?, 4.3: Basic Market Segmentation Criteria, and 4.7: Customer/Prospect Summary.)

6. *Market potential*
   (What size are the markets and what potential sales, profit, or other advantages does each have? See Figure 4.7: Customer/Prospect Summary.)

7. *How to achieve your goals*
   • Overall strategy
     (See Figure 10.6: Checklist for Strategic Planning.)
   • Competitive strategies
     (See Figure 5.7: Competitive Objectives.)
   • Promotion strategies
     (See Figure 9.5: Promotional Summary.)
   • Pricing, Place, Sales Practices
     (Brief statement of pricing strategy from Figure 6.4: Price Setting Thoughts, 6.5: Pricing Checklist, plus brief statements about location, hours, and selling practices from Chapter Six if important or changed from normal patterns.)
   • Marketing and advertising budgets
     (See Figure 2.8: Preliminary Marketing Budget Estimates and 9.5: Promotional Summary.)

8. *Potential problems*
   (Brief description, plus proposed solutions, from Figure 2.6: Problems.)

9. *Implementation and measurement of timetables and benchmarks*
   (See Figures 11.3: Marketing Action Plan and 11.4: Marketing Action Timetable.)

10. *Review and evaluation schedule*
    (Short schedule of important review dates.)

    Appendix: Include supporting documents such as letters of intent and purchase agreements, if you think documentation is needed.

MARKETING PLAN FOR R. D. MONTVILLE & ASSOCIATES

Mission Statement

R. D. Montville & Associates provides tax and management advisory services to local small business owners, helping them to grow and providing our employees with a rewarding working environment.

Marketing Objectives

Within one year, we plan to

- work on building our identity in the market;
- develop a database of businesses in the $700,000 to $5 million annual revenue range.

Within three years, we plan to

- develop more management consulting and do less traditional accounting;
- focus our business by specializing in the retail auto and related industries.

Sales and Profit Goals

	For next year	In three years
Consulting services	$85,000	$125,000
Monthly accounting	45,000	60,000
Audits	20,000	50,000
Tax returns	45,000	65,000
Tax consultation	45,000	55,000
Special projects	60,000	90,000
Other services	20,000	20,000
Sales goals:	320,000	500,000
Profit goals:	$48,000	$75,000

We feel that this is a conservative set of goals. Profit is likely to increase as a percentage of sales as we focus more closely on a select number of higher-level clients. If we were to increase our profit on sales to 20 percent next year's profit would be $64,000, a figure we think we can reach.

Products and Services

Business and management consulting. Providing overall financial management consulting for small businesses with revenues ranging from $700K–$5 million. We plan to increase this element of our business.

Monthly accounting services. Providing ongoing accounting services for a monthly fee. We plan to keep this element of our business flat.

Audits. Providing auditing services. This is currently a small part of our business, and we plan to keep it that way.

Tax return preparation. Completing tax returns for very small businesses and sole proprietors. We plan to de-emphasize this segment of our market. As we change our client mix we will bill substantially more for tax return preparation, consulting, and representation.

Special Projects. Providing complete financial management and accounting services for the automobile, motorcycle, and heavy equipment retailers. We plan to double our sales to this niche in the next three years.

Target Markets

Our best customers are those in the auto and related industries. With an average of $2 to $5 million in revenue, they can afford $10,000 to $25,000 in financial management services and are willing to pay an annual retainer. By specializing, we plan to be able to provide service tailored to this market, allowing us to dominate the niche as the "experts in advising auto dealerships."

Market Potential

There are 40 auto dealers in our immediate area, and we currently service 10 percent of that market. In addition, there are ten motorcycle dealerships, nine heavy equipment dealers, and four RV dealers. By increasing our market share of the auto dealers to 25 percent, we can add as much as $150K in revenue in three years. With 15 percent of the related dealers, we can add another $50K.

How We Will Achieve Our Goals

- *Overall strategy*. We will seek new markets for our most profitable services: financial and management consulting. We will concentrate on increasing our market share of the auto dealers, and go after motorcycle, RV, and heavy equipment dealers in our geographic area.
- *Competitive strategy*. We plan to build on our strengths in selling, production, and personnel, while attacking our competition's weaknesses: follow-up and narrow range of services. We will need to improve our finances by investing more of the profits into promotion, and by paying more attention to training our personnel.
- *Promotion strategies*. We plan to start an informational newsletter promoting our services and stressing our expertise in the auto-related market, our ties to the local area, and our commitment to the community. We will establish an informational home page linked to <www.portsmouthnh.com> and to the chambers of commerce home pages in our area. We will also establish links to auto dealer pages as we find them. The newsletter may be distributed electronically, providing an enhanced service to our target market. We will use the newsletter to build our identity in that niche and to build a database of all companies in our target market. We will sell them with a combination of direct mail, telephone follow-up, and brochures explaining the nature of our services. We will also support the other services we offer with yellow pages advertising and sponsorship of local events.

- *Pricing and sales practices.* Since our target market consists of growing commercial customers and our reputation is one of superior service and strong ties to the local community, we will continue to set our prices slightly above the cut-rate competition. (We can save our customers enough money to pay for our services.)

  But we will adopt a more aggressive sales approach. Having targeted the ideal market for our services (auto-related industry) we can pitch each potential customer with a direct mail, telephone follow-up, and personal presentation punch that should increase our market share.

- *Marketing and advertising budgets.* We will increase our investment in marketing and advertising to $42,000 annually. The breakdown is as follows:

Selling (direct costs)	$ 6,800
Selling (indirect costs)	8,500
Advertising	10,000
Direct sales, promotion	12,000
Public relations	600
Shipping and handling	2,400
Credit and collection	500
Marketing administration	1,200
TOTAL	**$42,000**

Potential Problems

From a marketing perspective, our biggest obstacle is time. We plan to overcome this by focusing our efforts on the auto-related niche and by adding another person to the staff in six months.

Another potential problem is aggressive competitors in the market. We are combating this with the marketing initiatives outlined in this plan.

Implementation and Measurement

Marketing Action Plan

By: _____   Date: _____

Strategic Objective: Focus on auto-related niche of the market.

Action Steps	Target Date	Person Responsible	Results
Identify all prospects and call on in reverse order of desirability three per week	6/15/03	G & B	
Create and mail first newsletter to prospect list	10/03	G & B	
Make proposals to ten prospects	11/03	G & B	
Close one prospect per month—three by end of year	12/03	G & B	
Home page improved and updated	3/03		

Marketing Action Timetable

By: _____   Date: _____

Action step: _____   Target Date: _____

Completed: _____   Not Completed but due: _____

List

Sub-step	Completion Criterion (Benchmark)	Dates of Completion
1. Check yellow pages	List of dealerships	5/15/03
2. Drive around and check for prospect	List of those not in yellow pages	5/22/03
3. Clip ads from all local newspapers	List those not found elsewhere	5/15/03
4. Input all prospects into database	Database set up, prospects listed	6/15/03
5. Home page	Up and running, links established	3/03

Review and Evaluation

At the end of the year, we will evaluate our progress as part of the planning and budgeting process for next year. At that time we will have a more accurate idea of how realistic our goals are and can reforecast based on our experience at that time.

MARKETING PLAN FOR DELICIOUS DELECTABLES

The following sample marketing plan was created with research done by Daniel DiSanti, Francine Cimaglio, and Timothy DeWolf using *The Market Planning Guide* in a course at Rhode Island College taught by Dr. Nadia J. Abgrab. Please note that each section of the plan is referenced to the appropriate worksheets contained in the book. As you create your own marketing plan, remember that the planning process is at least as important as the finished, written plan to the success of your business. Don't be tempted to simply write a plan based on this model without working through the book chapter by chapter—use the worksheets, then finalize your plan from the information you've gathered together. By following this process, you may even surprise yourself and discover new markets or approaches that you might have otherwise overlooked.

Marketing Plan for

Delicious Delectables

Not the Same Old Chocolates

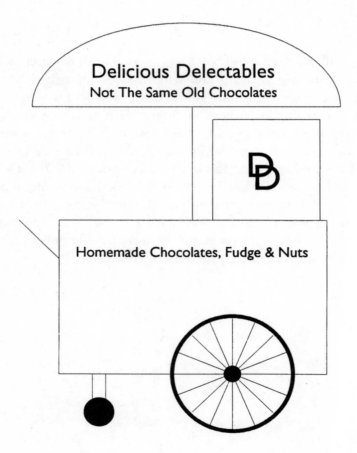

Mission Statement

To provide fresh-made, affordable, up-to-date chocolates and related food products for modern, up-to-date people, at a competitive price, in convenient locations, at a profit.

Marketing Goals for Next Year

1. Develop name brand loyalty and acceptance of Delicious Delectable (DD) products.
2. Expand into two malls (pushcarts).
3. Test expanded product lines.
4. Get better mall demographic and market data.

Long-Term Marketing Goals

1. Expand regionally; add mall sites.
2. Develop mail order business.

Sales and Profit Goals

- For next year: sales $260,000; profit pre-tax $45,000
- In three years: sales $680,000; profit pre-tax $172,000

Product Lines

Chocolates, nuts, fudge, gift packs, prepackaged chocolates (low-cost impulse items). These have the benefits of being affordable luxuries with a modern appeal: hip, upscale, affordable status products that taste good. Another benefit: the chocolates and fudge are made fresh daily.

Target Markets

Ages 17–40; image and status conscious middle/upper-middle-class buyers; mall walkers.

Market Potential

Average total weekly shopper flow of 210,000 (30,000 persons/day) in each mall (varies by season). In order to hit our sales projections, we will need to average 90 transactions per day (nine per hour) at $8 per sale, which represents less than one percent of the total market of mall shoppers.

Current Strategy,
Figure 10.3

Checklist for
Strategic Planning,
Figure 10.6

Comparing Yourself
to the Competition,
Figure 5.3

Quick Comparison,
Figure 5.4

Competitive
Objectives,
Figure 5.7

Advertising/
Promotional Goals,
Figure 9.3

Advertising/
Promotional
Questions,
Figure 9.6

Price Objectives,
Figure 6.1

Promotion Audit,
Figure 9.1

Advertising Base,
Figure 9.2

Problem Solving
Worksheet,
Figure 10.1

Marketing Action
Plan, Figure 11.3,
11.4

Overall Strategy

Develop and penetrate new markets (start-up) by offering products in contemporary shapes, today's popular colors, and designs to satisfy younger tastes. By offering them affordable products we hope to win their loyalty. The market will be attracted to the image our products portray.

Competitive Strategy

Delicious Delectables will distinguish itself in the market with fresh-daily product packaged and sold and made with care by individuals, not mass-produced.

Promotional Strategy

Our primary strategy is to locate the pushcarts in high-traffic areas of the malls. This means that much of the advertising is covered by the mall rental fees—we piggyback on the malls' advertising. Pushcart displays will feature our contemporary packaging and fresh approach. Sales personnel will be trained in friendly and courteous service. We'll offer free samples to introduce potential customers to our product. To build our customer database for future direct mail marketing, we will offer a premium for filling out and returning survey cards.

Pricing Strategy

We will position ourselves as an "affordable luxury." We will price our products higher than Fanny Farmer (the most direct competitor), but significantly below Godiva.

Marketing and Advertising Budgets

Most of our promotional efforts will be tied to our mall locations. (Rent = Space + Advertising!) $460/month space advertising, $200/month on giveaways. Sales commissions tied to sales levels.

Potential Problems

Start-up problems, new kids on the block. Entrenched competition (Fanny Farmer in the malls) and indirect competition (Godiva, other premium chocolates). Potential for new competition.

Timelines

1. Open first two sites; by 6/98; all partners.
2. Open third site by 3/99; all partners.
3. Research and test mail order by 6/98; send initial catalogs 10/98.

Delicious Delectables Inc.

Pro Forma

	Year 1	Year 2	Year 3	Total
Sales				
Chocolates	$108,000	$189,000	$283,500	$580,500
Fudge	50,400	88,200	132,300	270,900
Nuts	100,800	176,400	264,600	541,800
Gross Sales	**$259,200**	**$453,600**	**$680,400**	**$1,393,200**
Production Costs				
Chocolate (21%)	$22,680	$39,690	$59,535	$121,905
Fudge (39%)	19,656	34,398	51,597	105,651
Nuts (50%)	50,400	88,200	132,300	270,900
Total Production Cost	**$92,736**	**$162,288**	**$243,432**	**$498,456**
Net Sales	**$166,464**	**$291,312**	**$436,968**	**$894,744**
Expenses				
Rent	$47,000	$70,500	$70,500	$188,000
Advertising/promotion	5,528	5,528	35,527	46,582
Extra labor	9,288	32,688	53,488	95,464
Salaries	60,000	90,000	105,000	255,000
	$121,816	$198,716	$264,515	$585,046
Pretax Profits	$44,648	$92,596	$172,453	$309,698
Taxes at 40%	17,859	37,038	68,981	123,879
Add to R.E.	**$26,789**	**$55,558**	**$103,472**	**$185,819**

Delicious Delectables Customer Survey

To our valued customers:

Please take a few minutes to complete this questionnaire. Our aim is to give you the service you deserve. This questionnaire will help us serve our customers better.

1. How would you rate the quality of our products?
   Excellent _____ Good _____ Fair _____ Poor _____

2. How would you rate the quality of our service?
   Excellent _____ Good _____ Fair _____ Poor _____

3. How could we improve our products/service?
   _____
   _____
   _____

4. How did you become aware of Delicious Delectables?
   _____
   _____
   _____

5. Would you recommend Delicious Delectables to your friends?
   Yes _____ No _____

With your completed survey

10% off your next purchase at Delicious Delectables

Thank you for shopping at
Delicious Delectables
Rhode Island Mall
Warwick, Rhode Island

Emerald Square Mall
N. Attleboro, Massachusetts

Delicious Delectables
Not The Same Old Chocolates

Homemade Chocolates, Fudge & Nuts

Appendix

Rental Expense
Push carts: source is Wendy Smith, Emerald Square Mall

Non-holiday rates | Holiday rates
flat rates $1,500/mo. | 8 weeks (Nov.–Dec.) $8,500

Staffing requirements–all mall hours
Non-holiday staffing hours | Holiday staffing hours
M-Sa 10:00 AM–9:00 PM | graduating
Sun 12:00 AM–6:00 PM |
Total = 72 hours | Total = 85 hours

Annual rental expense, two pushcarts = $47,000

Production Costs

Product	Cost/lb.	Packaging	Total/lb.	Aver. selling price/lb.
Chocolate	$1.88	+10%	$2.07	$10.00
Fudge	$2.50	+10%	$2.75	$7.00
Nuts	$3.20	+10%	$3.52	$7.00

Annual Sales, Year 1
(Source: Judy, Fanny Farmer, Galleria Mall) sales per day

Product	lbs./day	dly x 2	Average price/lb.	Annual Gross Sales
Chocolate	15	30	$10.00	$108,000.00
Fudge	10	20	$7.00	$50,400.00
Nuts	20	40	$7.00	$100,800.00

Annual Sales, Year 2
+50% the addition of a third pushcart will increase sales 33%
        additional growth = 17%

Annual Sales, Year 3
+50% the addition of mail order will increase sales 30%
        natural growth of 20%

Labor Expense
(Source: Danny)

Year 1 Cost	Year 2 Cost	Year 3 Cost
Pt. time 30 hrs./wk/ $9,288.00	2 full time plus year 1 $32,688.00	1 full time chef+ $53,488.00

Promotion
(Source: Nadia)

Type	Year 1 Cost	Year 2 Cost	Year 3 Cost
Newsprint 1/8 page @ 62.60 year 3 add 30K printing exp.	$3,250.00	$3,250.00	$33,250.00
Giveaways Choc. 10 lbs./wk. Fudge 10 lbs./wk.	$2,277.60	$2,277.60	$2,277.60

5.3% of sales
(Source: Danny)

Product	% of sales	Fixed cost %	Variable cost %
Chocolate	42	41.6	26.8
Fudge	20	42.5	44.9
Nuts	38	40.3	55.6

Product	$Sales	Fixed Costs	Variable Costs
Chocolate	$108,000	$44,928	$28,944
Fudge	$50,400	$21,420	$22,630
Nuts	$100,800	$40,622	$56,045

WORKSHEETS

Appendix Four contains all the worksheets from *The Market Planning Guide's* text. Please feel free to photocopy these forms for your personal business use. Please respect our copyrights if you wish to reproduce them for republication. Contact us by writing to: Rights Dept., Dearborn Trade Publishing, 30 S. Wacker Drive, Suite 2500, Chicago, IL 60606-7481, or call us at 312-836-4400.

1. Name and date the business was established: _____

2. Check one: The business is a:
   ❏ corporation   ❏ Sub S or a Limited type corporation   ❏ partnership   ❏ sole proprietorship

3. Check one: Our customers are primarily:
   ❏ individuals   ❏ corporate   ❏ institutional   ❏ other (*describe briefly*) _____

4. Current products and services include _____

5. My five closest competitors are
   1.
   2.
   3.
   4.
   5.

6. Possible competition could come from:
   a. other companies:
   b. technologies:
   c. industries:

7. Allies actual or prospective include: _____
   _____

8. Is demand for my products or services increasing or decreasing?: _____
   _____

9. Products or services I might discontinue are _____
   _____

10. Products or services I might introduce are _____
    _____

11. Markets I might exit are _____
    _____

12. Markets I might enter are _____
    _____

13. My company is unique because _____
    _____

14. Right now my company's biggest marketing obstacle is _____
    _____

15. Our biggest marketing opportunity is _____
    _____

16. Our overall business goals and growth plans are _____
    _____

FIGURE 1.1 The Business Definition Worksheet

Use your completed Business Description Worksheet as your guide. Circle or otherwise highlight key phrases in Figure 1.1. Jot them down where you think they belong in the following categories. Write down the single most important goal for your business. Then condense the result into one or two short sentences. This will result in a mission statement that accurately reflects your business's purposes.

Customers: _____

_____

Products or services: _____

_____

Markets: _____

_____

Economic objectives: _____

_____

Beliefs, values, and aspirations: _____

_____

Distinctive competence: What are we *really* good at?: _____

_____

Concern for employees: _____

_____

Mission Statement

_____

_____

_____

_____

_____

_____

FIGURE 1.2 Mission Statement Worksheet

Factor	Strengths	Weaknesses
1.		
2.		
3.		
4.		
5.		
6.		
7.		
8.		
9.		
10.		
11.		
12.		
13.		
14.		
15.		
16.		
17.		
18.		
19.		
20.		

FIGURE 1.3 Internal Analysis: Strengths and Weaknesses

Factor	Opportunities	Threats
Current customers		
Prospect		
Competition		
Technology		
Political climate		
Government and other regulatory bodies		
Legal		
Economic environment		

FIGURE 1.4 External Analysis: Opportunities and Threats

The most important strengths we possess and the best opportunities we face are:

1. _____

2. _____

3. _____

4. _____

5. _____

The most dangerous weaknesses and threats we face are:

1. _____

2. _____

3. _____

4. _____

5. _____

FIGURE 1.5 SWOT Summary

To build on our major strengths and opportunities listed on Figure 1.5, we will take the following actions:

#1 Strength or opportunity

Action

#2 Strength or opportunity

Action

#3 Strength or opportunity

Action

FIGURE 1.6 Building on Strengths and Weaknesses

To shore up the weaknesses and avoid the threats listed on Figure 1.5, we will take the following actions:

#1 Weakness or threat

Action

#2 Weakness or threat

Action

#3 Weakness or threat

Action

FIGURE 1.7 Shore Up Weaknesses, Avoid Threats

Goal:

Person responsible:

Due date:

Goal:

Person responsible:

Due date:

Goal:

Person responsible:

Due date:

Goal:

Person responsible:

Due date:

FIGURE 1.8 Long-Term Goals

In order to achieve the goals set in Figure 1.8, break them down into short-term objectives to be accomplished within the next year:

Long-term goal #1:

Short-term objectives:

Long-term goal #2:

Short-term objectives:

Long-term goal #3:

Short-term objectives:

FIGURE 1.9 Turning Goals into Objectives

If you have many products or services, try to bundle them together into no more than ten categories. You can always expand the list later—but for now, keep it simple.

Product/Service	Target Markets
1.	
2.	
3.	
4.	
5.	
6.	
7.	
8.	

FIGURE 2.2 Product/Service and Market List

1. How much money do you want, or need, to earn?

_____

2. What sort of lifestyle is desirable for you and your family?

_____

3. How big do you want your business to become?

_____

4. How will your business reflect you and your values?

_____

5. How much risk do you want to take? In what areas?

_____

6. What do you want to achieve over the next five years?

_____

FIGURE 2.3 Personal Goals for the Business

Product	Worst Case	Most Likely Case	Best Case

FIGURE 2.4 Best Case/Worst Case Approach

Marketing Goals

1. _____
2. _____
3. _____
4. _____

Sales Goals for each Product/Service (see Figure 2.4 for next year's most likely figures)

	For next year	In three years
1. _____	_____	_____
2. _____	_____	_____
3. _____	_____	_____
4. _____	_____	_____
5. _____	_____	_____
6. _____	_____	_____
7. _____	_____	_____
Sales Goals	_____	_____
Profit Goals: ____% of sales	_____	_____

Comments:

_____
_____
_____

FIGURE 2.5 Preliminary Marketing, Sales, and Profit Goals

Today's date _____

What problems am I avoiding?

1. _____
2. _____
3. _____

What problems might prevent us from reaching our marketing, sales, and profit goals?

1. _____
2. _____
3. _____

What are we going to do about these problems? (See Figures 1.6 and 1.7.)

1. Assign responsibility to individuals to achieve solutions.

2. Allocate resources and authority to these people.

3. Establish benchmarks and deadlines to help them monitor their progress.

FIGURE 2.6 Problems

This is not an exhaustive list. Use it as a starting point. Your company will use some of these categories plus others peculiar to your marketing needs.

1. Selling (direct costs)

   Sales salaries and commissions $ _____

   Travel $ _____

   Entertainment $ _____

2. Selling (indirect costs)

   Training $ _____

   Marketing research $ _____

   Sales statistics $ _____

   Subscriptions and dues $ _____

3. Advertising $ _____

4. Sales promotion other than advertising $ _____

5. Public relations $ _____

6. Shipping and handling

   Order filling, packaging $ _____

   Postage and cartage $ _____

7. Credits and collection

   Administrative expense $ _____

   Bad debt allowance $ _____

8. Marketing administration $ _____

   Total $ _____

FIGURE 2.7 Marketing Budget Items

Made by:_____   Date:_____

Reviewed by: _____   Date: _____

Goal or Action	Timing	Annual Costs
TOTAL:		

FIGURE 2.8 Preliminary Marketing Budget Estimates

Basis for Wanting Things

	Applies	Doesn't Apply	Don't Know
To fill biological needs			
To gain security			
To get status			
To gain recognition			
To satisfy aggressions			
To satisfy sensibilities			
To lessen anxiety			
To save time			

Buyer Motivations

	Applies	Doesn't Apply	Don't Know
Satisfaction of the senses			
Imitation of others			
Style			
Profit			
Convenience			
Knowledge			
Comfort			
Fear			
Pride			
Curiosity			
Pleasure			
Self-expression or self-actualization			
Gaining an advantage			
Saving money			

Important Buying Factors for Institutional Markets

	Applies	Doesn't Apply	Don't Know
Dependability			
Discounts for bulk orders			
Price and quality			
Relationship with current vendors			
Customization			
Market exclusivity			
Value			
Delivery schedules			
Guarantees			
Safety for the purchasing agent			

FIGURE 3.1 Why Do People Buy Things?

Product/service

	Yours	The Competitions'
Target markets		
Benefits advertised/promoted		
Quality		
Price		
Improved versions		
Location		
Delivery		
Follow-up service		
Availability		
Convenience		
Reliability		
Service		
Guarantees		
Other (specify)		

FIGURE 3.2 Product Comparison Form

Product/service: _____

What are its features?   _____
_____

What benefits does it produce?   _____
_____

How is it used?   _____
_____

How is it purchased (unit, bulk, with other products)?   _____
_____

What are other possible applications of this product/service?   _____
_____

FIGURE 3.3 Product Application Worksheet

Your Product or Service	Benefits it Offers (Wants/Needs Fulfilled)	Possible Target Markets

FIGURE 3.4 Product/Service Benefits and Markets

Products with major impact on O & P:

Contributors	**Amounts**
1. _____	$ _____
2. _____	$ _____
3. _____	$ _____
4. _____	$ _____

Detractors	**Amounts**
1. _____	$ _____
2. _____	$ _____
3. _____	$ _____
4. _____	$ _____

FIGURE 3.5 Winners and Losers

Person responsible: _____   Review date: _____

Product/service idea: _____

_____

Benefits it will offer: _____

Target markets: _____

Timing: _____

Anticipated sales: ($ or unit; by quarter) _____

Anticipated costs:

    1. Development: _____

    2. Advertising: _____

    3. Impact on other products/services: _____

    4. Other (specify): _____

Comments: _____

_____

Action taken: _____

_____

By: _____   Date: _____

FIGURE 3.7 New Product/Service Objectives

Product/Service	1st Quarter	2nd Quarter	3rd Quarter	4th Quarter	Total
1.					
2.					
3.					
4.					
5.					
6.					
7.					
8.					
9.					
10.					
11.					
12.					
13.					
14.					
15.					

FIGURE 3.8 Summary of Product/Service Goals

Go through this exercise to gain a preliminary sense of the demographics of your target market. The reason to begin with "your best customers" is simple. Some people are better customers for you than others, and you presumably would want to find more customers like them. You may have a variety of best customers. Fine—go through this exercise for each customer group you feel is valuable to you. Don't dwell too long on this form. You will hone the information as you go along.

If you are a new business owner and have no customers yet, go ahead and imagine who your ideal customer would be.

1. Describe your best customers:
   age
   sex
   income level
   occupation
   If industrial or business:
   type of business (SIC)
   size

---

2. Where do they come from?
   (check one)

   ❏ local   ❏ regional
   ❏ national   ❏ international
   ❏ tourist

---

3. What do they buy?
   product(s)
   services
   benefits

---

4. How often do they buy?
   (check one)

   ❏ daily   ❏ weekly
   ❏ monthly   ❏ every now and then
   ❏ other

---

5. How much do they buy?
   Units
   Dollars

---

6. How do they buy? (check one)

   ❏ credit (you invoice them) ❏ cash
   ❏ contract

---

7. How did they learn about your business?
   (check all that apply)

   ❏ advertising: newspaper, radio/TV
   ❏ word of mouth   ❏ location
   ❏ direct sales   ❏ Internet
   ❏ other (specify)

---

8. What do they think of your
   business/products/services?
   (Customer perceptions)

---

9. What do they want you to provide
   (what benefits are they looking for that you
   can or should provide?)

FIGURE 4.1 Who Are Your Customers?

10. How big is your market?
    geographically
    population
    potential customers

11. What is your share of that market?
    (market share)

12. How do you want your markets to perceive your
    business?

FIGURE 4.1 Who Are Your Customers?, continued

Project or Bid (by customer)	Product or Service	Won or Lost?	Date	Reasons

FIGURE 4.2 Project or Bid Analysis

Use these categories as criteria to describe your customer base. Look for clusters of people described by these criteria; these help direct further marketing efforts. Your descriptions can be general. For example, Age range: 35–65; Gender: both; Income level: $60,000 and up.

Demographic
    Age range
    Gender
    Income level
    Occupation
    Religion
    Race/ethnic group
    Education
    Social class

Geographic
    Country
    Region
    State
    County
    City/town
    Size of population
    Climate
    Population density

Psychographic
    Leader or follower
    Extrovert or introvert
    Achievement-oriented or content with the status quo
    Independent or dependent
    Conservative or liberal
    Traditional or experimental
    Societally-conscious or self-centered

Consumer/Behavioral
    Rate of usage
    Benefits sought
    Method of usage
    Frequency of usage
    Frequency of purchase

Business Markets
    Type of business (manufacturer, retail, wholesale, service)
    Standard Industrial Classification (SIC) Code
    Size of business
    Financial strength
    Number of employees
    Location
    Structure
    Sales level
    Special requirements
    Distribution patterns

FIGURE 4.3 Basic Market Segmentation Criteria

Market Segment by Product or Service	Customers	Prospects

FIGURE 4.4 Market Segment Analysis

By: _____ Date: _____

Product: _____
_____

Describe your best customers (or ideal customer) according to the criteria listed in Figures 4.2 and 4.3: __
_____
_____

Describe their purchasing patterns: _____
_____
_____
_____
_____

What makes them the best or ideal customers for this product or service? _____
_____
_____

FIGURE 4.5 Market Segmentation Worksheet

To our valued clients:
Please take a few minutes to complete this short questionnaire. Out aim is to give you the service you need, want, and deserve. Your honest answers to these questions can help us serve you better.

1. How would you rate the quality of work we have performed for you in the past?

   Excellent _____   Good _____   Fair _____   Poor _____

   a. If not excellent, please explain.

   _____

   _____

2. How would you rate the timeliness of the work we perform for you?

   Excellent _____   Good _____   Fair _____   Poor _____

   a. If not excellent, please explain.

   _____

   _____

3. What service would you like us to perform for you that we do not offer?

   _____

   _____

4. Please feel free to give us any constructive criticism you feel we could use.

   _____

   _____

5. We plan to begin a seminar series in the not too distant future. What areas would you like to see covered in these seminars?

   _____

   _____

   a. How interested would you be in attending our seminars?

   Very _____   Somewhat _____   Little _____   Not at all _____

FIGURE 4.6 Client Survey

By: _____   Date: _____

Reviewed by: _____   Date: _____

These are our most valuable customers and prospects, ranked from the top. Make sure you list the market segments and their criteria.

Name of Customer	Market Segment	Criteria (Figure 4.3)
1.		
2.		
3.		
4.		

We should target these prospects

Name of Prospect	Market Segment	Criteria (Figure 4.3)
1.		
2.		
3.		
4.		

We should consider these market niches

1. _____

2. _____

3. _____

4. _____

Our customer/prospect objectives for the next year are

1. _____

2. _____

3. _____

4. _____

FIGURE 4.7 Customer/Prospect Summary Form

By:_____   Date: _____

My closest competitors are

1. _____

2. _____

3. _____

4. _____

5. _____

Other competitors (include indirect and potential competitors) are

1. _____

2. _____

3. _____

4. _____

5. _____

FIGURE 5.1 List of Competitors

Prepared by: _____   Date: _____

Competitor: _____

	Describe Your Competitor's	**How Do You Stack Up?**
Price		
Quality		
Service		
Location		
Advertising		
Other yardsticks		

FIGURE 5.3 Comparing Yourself to Competitors

Prepared by: _____ Date: _____

Competitor: _____

Product/service: _____

Location(s): _____

Specific information
    Years in business: _____
    Number of employees: _____
    Dollar sales: _____
    Unit sales: _____
    Market share: _____
    Financial strength: _____
    Profitability: _____

Players (include their ages, experience in this business, training or education, business strengths and weaknesses, and other pertinent information)
    President/owner: _____
    Key employees: _____
    Management capability: _____

The competition's marketing strategy
    Key customers: _____
    Major products or services: _____
    Quality: _____
    Image: _____
    Pricing: _____
    Advertising themes: _____
    Promotion/public relations efforts: _____

Significant changes (new people, products, etc.): _____

How this competitor competes with you: _____

Comments: _____

_____

_____

_____

_____

_____

_____

FIGURE 5.2 Competitor Information

	Competitor Offers	We Offer
Customer seeks:		
Quality		
Exclusivity		
Lower prices		
Product line		
Product service		
Reliability		
Delivery		
Location		
Information		
Availability		
Credit cards		
Credit line		
Warranty		
Customer advice		
Accessories		
Knowledgeability		
Polite help		

FIGURE 5.4 Quick Comparison

Strong — **+** | **−** — **Weak**

Where are you located on this continuum? What are you going to do about it?
How do you rank relative to the competition in these areas? A '+' means you are stronger than the competition, a '−' means you are weaker.

	Strong — +	− — Weak
Management		
Finances		
Marketing		
Pricing		
Selling		
Production		
Distribution		
Training		
Personnel		
Style/image		
Other		

FIGURE 5.5 Competitive Continuum

Competitor:				
Sales in $				
Market share				
Product lines				
Service lines				
Reputation				

FIGURE 5.6 Competitor Analysis Summary

Prepared by: _____   Date: _____

Reviewed by: _____   Date: _____

We need to improve our competitive position in the following areas:

1. _____

2. _____

3. _____

We can build on our competitive strengths in the following areas:

1. _____

2. _____

3. _____

We can attack our competition in the following weak areas:

1. _____

2. _____

3. _____

FIGURE 5.7 Competitive Objectives

By: _____   Date: _____

Product or service: _____

My Pricing Objectives	What Objective Will Accomplish	Time Frame for Reaching Objective

FIGURE 6.1 Pricing Objectives

The breakeven formula is:

$$BE = F/(S-V)$$

where   BE = breakeven sales in dollars

F = fixed costs in dollars

S = sales expressed as 100%

V = variable costs as a percentage of sales.

If F = $10,000, S = 100%, and V = 50%, Then BE = ($10,000/50%) = $20,000.

In other words, costs will exceed revenue until you have sold $20,000 worth of goods.

FIGURE 6.2 Breakeven Analysis

By: _____   Date: _____

Product/service: _____

Price range: $ _____ to $ _____

1. Price floor:
    (a) Markon (gross margin) is _____% of retail price.
    (b) Manufacturer's Suggested Price is $ _____.
    (c) Fixed costs are $ _____. Variable costs are $ _____
        or _____ percent of sales.
    (d) Breakeven is $ _____.

2. Special considerations for this product's price are:
    ❏ service
    ❏ status
    ❏ quality
    ❏ loss leader
    ❏ demand
    ❏ product life
    ❏ overhead
    ❏ downtime
    ❏ competition
    ❏ market penetration costs
    ❏ other (specify):

3. Turnover rate is _____ times per year.

4. Industry turn average is _____ times per year.

5. Going rate is _____.

6. I estimate _____ units will be sold.

7. _____ (number of units) at $ _____ will cover my fixed costs.

8. Top price possible is $ ____ . (This estimate is based on the customer's perception of value.)

Comments _____

_____

_____

_____

FIGURE 6.3 Price Range Guidelines

Consider setting prices above your competitor's prices if your	Yes	No	?
market is not sensitive to price changes			
market consists mainly of growing commercial customers			
product is an integral part of an established system			
reputation for status, service, and other positive perceptions in the market increases your product's perceived value			
customers can easily build your price into their selling price			
product is only a tiny percentage of your customers' total costs			

Consider setting your prices just below your competition if	Yes	No	?
your market is very sensitive to price changes			
you're attempting to enter a new market			
your customers need to reorder parts or supplies			
your business is small enough that a lower price won't threaten your larger competitors and start a price war			
you have the option of economical production runs which decrease your unit cost			
you have not reached full production capacity			

FIGURE 6.4 Price Setting Thoughts

Estimating demand

1. Which products/services do customers shop around for? _____
2. Which products/services are in greater demand even at higher prices? _____
   _____
3. Are certain products/services in greater demand at one time of the year than another? If so, which? And what is the duration of the demand? _____
4. Do your customers expect a certain price range? _____
5. What is the balance between price and quality in your market? _____
   _____

The competition

1. What are your competitor's pricing strategies? _____
2. Are your prices based on an average gross margin consistent with your competition's? _____
   _____
3. Is your policy to sell consistently at a higher price, lower price, or the same price as your competitors? Why? _____
4. How do competitors respond to your prices? _____
   _____

Pricing and market share

1. What is your present market share? _____
2. What are your market share goals? To increase share? Maintain share? _____
   _____
3. What effect will price changes have on your market share? _____
   _____
4. Is your production capacity consistent with your market share goals? _____
   _____

Strategy

1. Have you determined how pricing affects your sales/volume goals? _____
   _____
2. How can pricing help you gain new business? _____
   _____
3. Have you tested the impact of price strategies on your markets? _____
4. Are your strategies in line with broader economic trends? _____

Policies

1. How does the nature of your products/services affect their price? _____
   _____
2. How does your method of distribution affect price? _____
3. Do your promotional policies affect prices? _____

FIGURE 6.5 Pricing Checklist

You need two traffic counts, one for pedestrians and one for vehicular traffic. You should find out

❑ how many people pass by during your business hours;

❑ when they pass by;

❑ who these people are;

❑ where they are from;

❑ what their shopping plans might be;

❑ how many are logical prospects for your products or services;

❑ if there are seasonal or other predictable fluctuations;

❑ where they currently buy your kind of products or services.

These pieces of information help you to evaluate your site. Your advertising and other promotional programs also need this information.

FIGURE 7.1 Traffic Counts

By:_____ Date: _____

Competitor: _____

Location: _____

Rate 1 (poor) to 5 (excellent)	Rating	Comments
1. Appearance and design of store		
2. Employees' characteristics		
A. Telephone manners		
B. Courtesy		
C. Helpfulness		
D. Appearance		
E. Product knowledge		
F. Ability to handle complaints		
G. Ability to cross-sell		
3. Availability of products		
4. Convenience of location		
5. Added services (delivery etc.)		
6. Other (specify):		

FIGURE 7.3 Shopping Competition (Including Yourself)

By:_____   Date: _____

1. How does the site affect your business? _____
   _____

2. How does the appearance of the building affect your business? _____
   _____

3. Does the store's or office's appearance complement your business's image? _____
   _____

4. Do you (or can you) use the location to your best advantage? How? _____
   _____

5. Should you move or consider moving? Why? _____
   _____

6. Is the neighborhood changing? If so, how? How will it affect your business? _____
   _____

7. Is the site high- or low-rent? _____
   _____

8. Is the rent competitive for the area? _____
   _____

9. If your site is low-rent, how will you attract customers? _____
   _____

10. Is the location good from a competitive viewpoint? _____
    _____

11. Is the traffic sufficient for your sales objectives? _____
    _____

12. Will neighboring stores help draw customers? _____
    _____

13. Is parking adequate? Would paying for customer parking make sense? _____
    _____

14. Can you develop additional traffic? How? _____
    _____

15. What disadvantages does the site have? How will you overcome them? _____
    _____

16. Is this the best site available for your business? If no, why not? _____
    _____

FIGURE 7.2 Site Evaluation

By: _____   Date: _____

Product or service: _____

My Pricing Objectives	What Objective Will Accomplish	Time Frame for Reaching Objective
1.		
2.		
3.		
4.		
5.		
6.		
7.		

FIGURE 7.4 Pricing Objectives

By: _____   Date: _____

Product or service: _____

My Pricing Objectives	What Objective Will Accomplish	Time Frame for Reaching Objective
1.		
2.		
3.		
4.		
5.		
6.		
7.		

FIGURE 7.5 Sales Practice Objectives

By:_____   Date: _____

Based upon your analysis of the business, the operation is being run satisfactorily in the area of:

	Yes	No
I. Sales and Marketing		
A. Pricing		
Are prices in line with current industry practice?		
Is your pricing policy based on your cost structure?		
Have you conducted price sensitivity studies?		
B. Market research		
Have you identified target markets?		
Do you segment your markets?		
Have you identified customer wants/needs?		
Do you know how your markets perceive your products?		
Has your business taken advantage of market potential?		
Has the competition been analyzed?		
C. Personal selling		
Do you know what your sales practices are?		
Does personal style influence your sales practices?		
D. Customer service		
Is customer service a priority?		
Do you solicit customer feedback?		
Is there a rational balance between serving your customer's needs and good business practice?		
E. Advertising and public relations		
Do you select media for measurable results?		
Is your advertising consistent?		
Does your advertising budget make sense in terms of the level of business and its anticipated, planned growth?		
F. Sales management		
Are salespersons and outside agents properly directed in their duties?		
Do you establish individual sales goals?		
Do you provide adequate sales support?		
Are your salespersons trained?		
G. Market planning		
Do you have a marketing budget?		
Do you have a market plan?		
Has your business taken advantage of market opportunities?		

FIGURE 8.1 Management Audit

	Yes	No
II. Business Operations		
A. Purchasing		
Are reputable, competitive vendors used?		
Do you have a purchasing program?		
B. Inventory control		
Do you know your inventory turn?		
Is slow-moving stock managed?		
Have you established rational reordering policies?		
C. Scheduling		
Do goods and materials move through the business without tie-ups and problems?		
Do you know how long each job should take?		
D. Quality control		
Are inferior incoming materials returned to vendors?		
Are reject rates minimized?		
Do you have a "do it right the first time" policy?		
E. Business growth		
Has your business grown at least above the rate of inflation?		
Have you met your asset growth, sales, and profit goals?		
F. Site location		
Do you have the right business site?		
G. Insurance		
Do you have an annual insurance review?		
Are the proper risks to your business (including yourself) covered?		
Do you put your insurance package out to bid every year?		
III. Financial		
A. Bookkeeping and accounting		
Are your books adequate?		
Are records easy to access?		
Can you get information when you need it?		
Do you have monthly P&Ls (income statements)?		
Do you have annual financial statements?		
B. Budgeting		
Do you use a cash flow budget?		
Do you use deviation analysis monthly?		
Are capital equipment purchases budgeted?		

FIGURE 8.1 Management Audit

	Yes	No
C. Cost control		
Are cost items managed?		
Are high cost items treated separately?		
Is the budget used as the primary cost control tool?		
D. Raising money		
Have you been successful in raising capital when it was needed?		
E. Credit and collection		
Do you use credit to judiciously increase revenues?		
Do you know your credit and collection costs?		
Is your current policy successful?		
Do you review credit and collection policies regularly?		
Do you have a receivables management policy?		
F. Dealing with banks		
Is your relationship with your lead banker open and friendly?		
Do you use more than one bank?		
G. Cost of money		
Do you compare the cost of money (interest, points) with your profit ratios?		
Are interest rates and loan conditions appropriate?		
H. Specific tools:		
Do you know and use:		
1) Break-even analysis?		
2) Cash flow projections and analysis?		
3) Monthly P&Ls (income statements)?		
4) Balance sheets?		
5) Ratio analysis?		
6) Industry operating ratios?		
7) Tax planning?		
IV. Personnel		
A. Hiring		
Has the right mix of people been hired?		
Do you hire from a pool of qualified applicants?		
Do you maintain a file of qualified applicants?		
B. Training		
Are your employees suitably trained for their jobs?		
C. Motivating people		
Do your employees appear to enjoy what they are doing?		

FIGURE 8.1 Management Audit, continued

	Yes	No
D. Enforcing policies		
Does there seem to be logic and order to what goes on in the business?		
Are reviews and evaluations performed on schedule?		
E. Communicating		
Are people informed and brought in on decisions?		
Do you create opportunities for employees to set their own goals?		
V. Administrative Management		
A. Record keeping		
Are records of past transactions and events easy to find?		
Are records retained for at least the minimum legal time period?		
Is access to personnel files limited?		
B. Problem solving		
Are there few unresolved problems?		
C. Decision making		
Are you decisive?		
Is there a decision process (chain of command)?		
D. Government regulations		
Are you aware of local, state, and federal regulations that affect your business?		
E. Leadership		
Do you actually take charge of the business and its employees?		
F. Developing subordinates		
If you were to die or be suddenly disabled, is there a ready successor?		
G. Business law		
Do you have a working knowledge of applicable business law: contracts, agency, Uniform Commercial Code, etc.?		
Do you know how current contracts and other legal obligations affect your business?		
H. Dealing with professionals		
Do you have and use an accountant, attorney, business consultant?		
Do you use outside advisors?		

FIGURE 8.1 Management Audit, continued

	Yes	No
I. We operate with a complete and up-to-date business plan which includes:		
A. One and three year projections		
B. A capital budget		
II. We operate with an annual marketing plan which includes:		
A. Precise sales and profit goals and timetables		
B. Strategies and tactics for the next three years		
C. Budgets, forecasts, and benchmarks		
D. A tentative sales plan		
Our marketing plan also includes:		
E. The demographics of our target markets		
F. A thoughtful definition of the markets we serve		
G. A definition of the needs/wants our products and services fill		
H. An analysis of the growth potential of our markets		
I. A competitive analysis		
J. A definition of our "Unique Selling Proposition"		
K. Projections for other products or services that could be developed		
L. Timetables for research and development		
III. We use monthly budgets and statements which include:		
A. Thorough and up-to-date records		
B. Cash flow budget		
C. P&L (income) statement		
D. Balance sheet		
E. Deviation analysis		
F. Ratio analysis		
G. Standard cost comparisons		
H. Cash reconciliation		
IV. We have developed an information base that allows us to:		
A. Keep track of new developments in the industry		
B. Obtain and study key trade information		
C. Understand what "state of the art" means in this business		
D. Provide customers with the best available information pertaining to our products and services		
E. Keep all our employees adequately informed		
V. I'm certain that the business is properly capitalized since I:		
A. Base capitalization on worst-case planning		
B. Have emergency funds (or access to them)		
C. Have discussed this with our commercial banker		

FIGURE 8.2 Good Management Scorecard

	Yes	No
VI. I understand the value of the business because I've made use of:		
A. Professional appraisers		
B. Present value methods to evaluate terms		
C. Professional tax planning counsel		
D. Accurate, timely financial information		
VII. We strive to improve production, quality and operations by:		
A. Keeping the plant in top condition		
B. Maintaining safe conditions		
C. Establishing high standards		
D. Standing behind our products and services		
E. Not tolerating shoddy performance		
F. Working for consistency		
G. Using our company's "look" as a statement to our markets		
VIII. Personnel decisions are based on humane, carefully considered policies which include:		
A. Checklists to make sure objectives are clear		
B. Communication, to make sure objectives are understood		
C. Written job descriptions		
D. Regular progress and performance evaluations		
E. Fair hiring practices		
F. Fair wage scales		
IX. As for my own personal/managerial skills, I work hard to:		
A. Develop my problem-solving abilities		
B. Always stay calm		
C. Be objective		
D. Avoid investments in my own ego		
E. Listen to my employees		
F. Plan changes in our course to minimize negative effects		
G. Make decisions promptly		
H. Always get the facts behind problems		
I. Accept my own limitations		
J. Delegate tasks that can be done more efficiently by someone else		
K. Analyze all available options		
L. Develop my reading/study habits		
M. Improve my skills		
N. Consider and evaluate risks		
O. Be positive with customers, employees, associates		

FIGURE 8.2 Good Management Scorecard, continued

Factor	Opportunities	Threats
Current customers		
Prospect		
Competition		
Technology		
Political climate		
Government and other regulatory bodies		
Legal		
Economic environment		

FIGURE 8.3 External Analysis: Opportunities and Threats Revisited

By: _____   Date: _____

Our most important strengths and best opportunities are:

1. _____
2. _____
3. _____
4. _____

Our most dangerous weaknesses and threats are:

1. _____
2. _____
3. _____
4. _____

FIGURE 8.4 Strengths and Weaknesses

#1 Weakness or threat

Action

#2 Weakness or threat

Action

#3 Weakness or threat

Action

#4 Weakness or threat

Action

FIGURE 8.5 Shore Up Weaknesses, Avoid Threats

#1 Strength or opportunity

Action

#2 Strength or opportunity

Action

#3 Strength or opportunity

Action

#4 Strength or opportunity

Action

#5 Strength or opportunity

Action

#6 Strength or opportunity

Action

#7 Strength or opportunity

Action

FIGURE 8.6 Build on Strengths, Seize Opportunities

By:_____   Date: _____

	Yes	No
Do you:		
Know where new business is coming from?		
Keep track of referrals and thank the sources?		
Track advertising and direct mail responses?		
Spend advertising dollars in proportion to your product mix?		
Project a strong, consistent image in all materials, signage, stationery, and so forth?		
Have a professionally designed logo?		
Sell benefits to customers in all promotional material?		
Know what has worked, what has not worked, and why?		
Have a yearly advertising, public relations, and promotion plan?		
Involve your entire staff in the promotional process?		
Advertise to your staff as well as to your markets?		
Have strong relationships with media people and advertising professionals in your community?		
Have a qualified in-house advertising/promotional person?		
Assign one person to make sure your plan is implemented?		
Have a professionally designed "facilities brochure" which explains what your business is?		
Follow up promotional efforts with one-on-one selling (if appropriate)?		
Have professional window and point-of-purchase displays?		
Have an appropriate Internet presence?		
Analyze your probable competition in connection with the direct and indirect sales promotional methods you use?		

For any "no" or "?" answer, you have another reason to use a professional advertising/public relations/promotion agency.

FIGURE 9.1 Promotion Audit

A successful promotional campaign requires answers to these six questions:

1. *Who?* Who are your customers and prospects? You have already segmented your markets, so you can describe who the promotion is aimed at. See Figure 4.1 in Chapter 4._____

   _____

   _____

2. *Why?* What are you trying to accomplish? Increase sales? Introduce a new product? Retain or increase market share? Create or maintain an image? See Question 25 in this chapter. _____

   _____

   _____

3. *When?* Timing in advertising is all-important. The best promotion will bomb if the timing is off. _____

   _____

   _____

4. *What?* What specific products or services are you trying to move? What is their unique selling proposition?

   _____

   _____

5. *Where?* What media would be best for your campaign?_____

   _____

   _____

6. *How?* Leave this one to your advertising agency. You have enough to do running your business. You have to review and approve the campaign. _____

   _____

   _____

The details—the "where" and "how"—are less important than getting your message out. Your ad agency will save you a lot of time here, help you make the right choices—and make the deadlines. Many good campaigns are sabotaged by well-intentioned business owners who know a lot about their business but little about advertising and promotion. Unfortunately, everyone thinks he or she is a good copywriter and art director. Nothing could be further from the truth.

FIGURE 9.2 Advertising Base

These are goals some astute small-business owners have set for their advertising and promotional campaigns. This is intended as a nudge to your thinking, not as a comprehensive list of goals.

Do you want to

- penetrate specialized markets? Which ones? What are the measures of progress (unit sales, dollar sales, benchmarks)? _____

_____

- sell more to present customers? How? _____

_____

- specialize in terms of product or services? Which ones? Why? _____

_____

- change your business's image? How? Why? To what? _____

_____

- penetrate geographical markets more deeply? Which areas? How? _____

_____

- create "top of mind" awareness? How? _____

_____

- expand demographically? To whom? What market segments? _____

_____

- increase sales of specific products or services? How? _____

_____

- announce new product, new product mix, or new location? _____

_____

- support community projects for public relations benefits? _____

_____

Your answers to these questions decide how you want to be perceived, whom you plan to do business with, and what you want to sell.

FIGURE 9.3 Advertising/Promotion Goals

Promotion encompasses a wide range of activities. Some will be appropriate for your business and your markets; some will not.

Paid Advertising

- ❏ Radio
- ❏ Television
- ❏ Internet

Print

- ❏ Newspapers
- ❏ Magazines
- ❏ "Shoppers" (free or classified ad magazines)
- ❏ Yellow pages
- ❏ Local telephone directories
- ❏ Special directories (regional, seasonal, chamber of commerce)
- ❏ Trade or industry directories (e.g.: *Thomas' Register of Manufacturers*)
- ❏ Cooperative or "co-op" ad support from your vendors
- ❏ Transportation advertisements (subways, busses)
- ❏ Billboards

Direct Mail

- ❏ Letters
- ❏ Newsletters
- ❏ Sales or product/service announcements
- ❏ Flyers
- ❏ Postcards
- ❏ "Special customer" offers
- ❏ Brochures
- ❏ Direct response
- ❏ Internet newsletter
- ❏ Coupons
- ❏ Bill stuffers

Public Relations

- ❏ News releases
- ❏ Articles in magazines, journals, etc.
- ❏ Open houses
- ❏ Speaking engagements
- ❏ Interview shows
- ❏ Sponsorship of community events and activities
- ❏ Seminars
- ❏ Workshops
- ❏ Service club membership and participation
- ❏ Other club memberships

FIGURE 9.4 Promotion Smorgasbord

Telemarketing
- ❑ Inquiry handling
- ❑ Direct marketing by phone
- ❑ Service: customer complaints, follow-up, special offers

One-on-one selling
- ❑ Presentation materials
- ❑ Personal letters
- ❑ Customized proposals
- ❑ Some telemarketing
- ❑ Sales personnel training

Sales promotions
- ❑ Discounts
- ❑ Loss leaders
- ❑ Coupons
- ❑ "Buy one, get one free"

Specialty advertising
- ❑ Matchbooks, key chains, and other novelties
- ❑ Calendars
- ❑ Date books

Facilities
- ❑ Site location and shared advertising
- ❑ Signage
- ❑ Window displays
- ❑ Point-of-purchase
- ❑ Fixtures and layout of store
- ❑ Lighting

Other types of promotion
- ❑ Flyers
- ❑ Posters
- ❑ Handouts
- ❑ Blimps and balloons
- ❑ Sandwich boards

Choosing the right promotional mix for your business calls for professional skills.
Check with your advertising and/or public relations agency.

FIGURE 9.4 Promotion Smorgasbord, continued

Type of Promotion	Audiences Targeted			Target Date	Estimated Costs
Advertising: newsletter and/or magazine					
Advertising: radio and/or television					
Advertising: other					
Home page or other Internet presence					
Direct mail					
Newsletter					
Yellow pages					
Flyers and brochures					
Public relations: press releases					
Sponsorship					
Open house or other special event					
Specialty items (e.g., matchbooks, T-shirts)					
Seminars or workshops					
Telemarketing					
Other					

FIGURE 9.5 Promotional Summary

Ask and answer these questions:

1. Markets
   What is your market mix?
   What percentage of your business comes from:
      individuals?
      small businesses?
      big businesses?
      local trade?
      regional trade?
      national or international trade?

2. Products/services
   Are your products:
      innovative?
      specialized?
      diversified?
      commodity?
      packaged?
      tailor-made or customized?
   (Answer "how" to each yes answer.)

3. Image
   Would you describe your business as:
      formal?
      informal?
      community focus?
      regional or national focus?
      aggressive?
      relaxed or laid-back?
      sophisticated?
      "down-home"?
      specialized?
      generalist?

   Does that description fit the way you want to be perceived, as well as the way you see yourself now?
   Or do you want to change your company's image?

4. Business strengths
   What special expertise, experience, and interests do you enjoy?
      longevity in the community?
      convenient location?
      outstanding service reputation?
      other: (specify)

5. Competition
   How do you stack up against your competition:
      market share
      image

FIGURE 9.6 Advertising/Promotional Questions

6. Customer base
Do you sell:
    many products and services to a few loyal customers?
    several products to a narrowly defined industry?
    single products to a diverse client base?

Do you have a database to tell you:
    product mix for each customer?
    where their business came from? (referral, advertising, etc.)
    basic demographics of your markets?

FIGURE 9.6 Advertising/Promotional Questions

Questions to ask when shopping for an advertising or public relations agency:

1. *What process does your agency use in analyzing client needs?* _____
_____

2. *Once you've determined my needs, what is the process used to position my company?* _____
_____

3. *How do you measure how effective your strategies are?* _____
_____

4. *How do you keep us informed about your activities?* _____
_____

5. *Who else have you worked with, especially similar to firms like mine? What success (and horror) stories do you have? Who may we contact?* _____
_____

6. *Describe a successful program for a business like ours. What were the goals of the program? What strategies and tactics did you use? How did you measure your success?* _____
_____

7. *If the campaign is Public Relations (PR or unpaid advertising), what are your relationships with the media? Are you on a first-name basis with "influencers" in our field?* _____
_____

8. *How do you approach creativity? How do you measure it? How do you involve clients in the creative process?* _____
_____

9. *What important clients have you lost in the past year? Why did you lose them? May I speak with them?* _____
_____

10. *Most important of all: Who will be working on our account day-by-day?* _____
_____

FIGURE 9.7 Selecting a Promotional Pro

	Print Ad	Two-Color Brochure	Coupon	Letter/Press Release
Choose publication				
Assign tasks/hire professionals				
Write				
Edit				
Design				
Get estimates for printing/choose printer				
Photography				
Illustration				
Paste-up				
Printing/proofing				
Total time				

FIGURE 9.8 Production Timelines

Please list the newspapers you read regularly.

	Daily	Weekly
1. First choice		
2. Second choice		
3. Third choice		

Please list the radio stations you listen to regularly.

1. First choice _____
2. Second choice _____
3. Third choice _____
4. Fourth choice _____
5. Fifth choice _____

Have you recently seen or heard our advertising?
Where? _____

Thank you for your help!
Your Logo

FIGURE 9.10 Ten-Second Media Quiz

By: _____   Date: _____

1. What is the problem? Cite standard and deviation from standard if available.

   _____

   _____

2. Possible causes:

   _____

   _____

3. Interim solution:

   _____

   _____

   _____

FIGURE 10.1 Problem Solving Worksheet

Your Current Strategy	Aggressive or Defensive?	Active or Passive?	Goal-Oriented or Opportunistic?
Marketing			
Management			
Financial			
Production			
Operations			

FIGURE 10.3 Current Strategy

Personal goals include nonfinancial goals as well as financial goals. Limit the goals to the most important.

Most Important Personal Goals

-
-
-
-
-

Business Goals

	Next Year	**Three Years**
Quantitative goals		
• Sales ($)		
• Sales (unit)		
• Profit ($)		
• Profit (% sales)		
• Market share		
• Company net worth ($)		
• Number of employees		
Qualitative goals		
• Market position		
• Kind of business		
• Target markets		
• Business culture or style		
• Other (specify):		

Potential conflicts between personal and business goals

_____

_____

Comments

_____

_____

FIGURE 10.2 Personal and Business Goal Summary

This checklist presents a range of small business strategic options proven in hundreds of applications.

Past	Current	Future	Strategy	Probable Consequences, Risks
			Sample Marketing Strategies	

FIGURE 10.6 Checklist for Strategic Planning

Past	Current	Future	Strategy	Probable Consequences, Risks
			Sample Marketing Strategies	
			Sample Financial Strategies	

FIGURE 10.6 Checklist for Strategic Planning, continued

Past	Current	Future	Strategy	Probable Consequences, Risks
			Sample Financial Strategies	
			Sample Production Strategies	
			Sample Operating Strategies	

FIGURE 10.6 Checklist for Strategic Planning, continued

These are the four Ps of marketing. Make sure the aspects of each variable pertaining to your business complement one another.

Product/service

New, modified, new application
Position on life cycle
    Cash cow?
    Rising star?
    Dog?
    Problem child?
Benefits to purchaser
Perceived value
Will products/services be bundled or sold individually?
What is the product mix?

Price

To end user
To distributors and to trade
    (What margins do you allow distributors and trade?)
Image
Market penetration
Market's sensitivity to price changes
Premium, skim, meet market rates, penetrate?

Place

Will you sell direct or through agents, wholesalers, or other intermediaries?
Location
Signs
Direct mail
Direct sales
Telemarketing

Promotions

What mix of media will you use?
Advertising (including yellow pages, classified ads)
Internet
Public relations
Trade shows
Packaging
Special promotions (sales, spotlights, etc.)
Direct mail
Personal or direct selling
Sales force training
Marketing support
Image: point-of-purchase, layout, lighting, stocking
Personal letters
Circulars, brochures, flyers

FIGURE 11.1 The Four Strategic Marketing Variables

By: _____   Date: _____

Action Steps	Target Date	Person Responsible	Results

FIGURE 11.3 Marketing Action Plan

By: _____ Date: _____

Action step: _____ Target date: _____

Completed: _____ Not completed but due: _____

List:

Sub-step	Completion Criterion (Benchmark)	Dates of Completion
1.		
2.		
3.		
4.		
5.		
6.		
7.		
8.		
9.		

FIGURE 11.4 Marketing Action Timetable

RESOURCES

Marketing

Guerrilla Marketing, 3/e by Jay Conrad Levinson (Mariner Books, 1998)

Target Marketing, 3/e by Linda Pinson and Jerry Jinnett (Dearborn Trade, 1996)

Periodical

Inc. One of the leading small business magazines. 38 Commercial Wharf, Boston, MA 02110 617-248-8000. $19/year.

Demographics

Census Catalog & Guide
U.S. Government Printing Office
732 North Capitol St., NW
Washington, DC 20402
202-512-0000

Statistical Abstract of the United States
U.S. Government Printing Office
732 North Capitol St., NW
Washington, DC 20402
202-512-0000
(Annual) $38

Importing and Exporting

A Basic Guide to Exporting
U.S. Government Printing Office
732 North Capitol St., NW
Washington, DC 20402
202-512-0000

Exporters' Encyclopedia
Dun & Bradstreet Information Services
Dun & Bradstreet Corporation
3 Sylvan Way
Parsippany, NJ 07054-3896
800-526-0651

Home-Based Business

Launching Your Home-Based Business by **David H. Bangs, Jr. and Andi Axman** (Dearborn Trade, 1997)

Working Solo, 2/e by **Teri Lonier** (John Wiley & Sons, 1998)

Surefire Strategies for Growing Your Home-Based Business by **David Schaefer** (Dearborn Trade, 1997)

American Home Business Association
4505 S. Wasatah Blvd.
Salt Lake City, UT 84124
800-664-2422
<www.homebusiness.com>

Manufacturing

Business Plan for Small Manufacturers
U.S. Small Business Administration
Office of Business Development
SBA Publications
<www.sba.gv/library/pubs.html#mp-4>

Service Industry

Service Industries USA: Industry Analyses, Statistics, and Leading Organizations, 4/e (Gale Group, 1998)

Sourcebooks

Small Business Sourcebook, 15/e by **Robert J. Elster** (Gale Group, 2001)

Encyclopedia of Associations, 38/e by Kimberly N. Hunt (Gale Group, 2001)

Government and Miscellaneous Associations

U.S. Chamber of Commerce
1615 H Street NW
Washington, DC 20062
202-463-5580

U.S. Consumer Information
U.S. Government Printing Office

732 North Capitol St., NW
Washington, DC 20402
202-512-0000

Library of Congress
101 Independence Avenue, SE
Washington, DC 20540
<www.loc.gov>

Small Business Service Bureau
546 Main Street
Worcester, MA 01608
508-756-3513

Small Business Administration
409 Third Street, SW
Washington, DC 20416
202-205-6600
<www.sba.gov>

Internet

Two online bookstores which allow you to search for books by topic, author or title:

Amazon
A favorite online bookstore. A vast selection of titles, author interviews, lists of books by author, field, genre, and lots more. Worth visiting even if you don't buy books!

Powell's Bookstore—used, new, and out of print
<www.powells.com>
Another online bookstore, with many unusual titles that are hard to find elsewhere.

Here are some of my favorite business-oriented Web sites. Most are self-explanatory; some need more information to be useful to you!

Adam Home Page
<www.ucomics.com/adamathome>

Some comic relief for us home workers.

American Home Business Association
One of the better home business associations

About Work: Ask the Experts
<www.aboutwork.com/experts>
Chats and bulletin boards run by experts.

American Demographics / **Marketing Tools**
Books, publications, resources, research tools, links. This is *the* site for
   market research.

American Express
<www.americanexpress.com/smallbusiness/>
Lots of good small business how-to information, monthly articles on specialized topics, and a long list of references to other sites of interest.

Apple Small Biz Site
<www.apple.com/smallbusiness>
Some how-to information, especially helpful for us Mac aficionados.
   Expert advice, links, success stories.

Better Business Bureau
<www.bbb.org>
The ethical watchdog. Does everything the old BBB did, but quicker.

Business@Home
<www.gohome.com>

Claris Small Business
<www.claris.com/smallbiz/>
Generally a good site. Some how-to; some expert advice. Includes share-
   ware templates for many business functions.

D&B Company Information
<www.hocmag.net>
Worth a visit. You can get business credit info, but at a cost.

Dearborn Publishing Group, Inc.
<www.dearborn.com>
My publishers, bless their hearts!

Digital Daily Welcome—IRS
<www.irs.ustreas.gov/prod/>
Welcome to the IRS. They really are trying to be more user-friendly.
   Contains updated information and a strong section on taxes for small
   business.Digital Daily Welcome—IRS

Home Based and Small
Business Resource Center
<http://members.tripod.com/~WorkinMoms/>
Newsletter, kids, parents working at home site. Chatty and fun for the
   work-at-home mother.

Home Page, Survey Research Center
<www.princeton.edu/~abelson/index.html>
A spectacular site if you need to develop a survey.

HR in a Box Home Page

<www.ultranet.com>

Sylvia Ho is a human resources lawyer. She's an entrepreneur—and her site is superb. A must-visit for any personnel or human resources question.

SalesLeadsUSA

<www.abii.com>

Khera Communications

<www.kciLink.com/>

Great free info on marketing, finance, and other matters. Locally focused (Washington, DC area) but with a much wider appeal.

Microsoft's Small Business Page

<www.bcentral.com>

Similar to Apple and Claris: good how-tos and links to other sites. Frequently updated.

National SBDC Research Network Homepage

<www.smallbiz.suny.edu>

Puts the research capabilities of the SBDC's nationwide network to work for you.

Small Business Administration

<www.sbaonline.sba.gov/>

The Small Business Administration is the first place any small business owner should visit. Their range of services—from counseling to financial guarantees—is very impressive. With the advent of the Small Business Development Center program, their quality rocketed upwards. Any entrepreneur who ignores this resource is being willfully self-destructive.

Small Business Advancement Center (University of Arkansas)

<www.sbaer.uca.edu/>

This site is a sleeper. It's full of gems: marketing tips, financing ideas, links, and more. A must-visit site. Even has a fine search engine built into it.

Survey Research Center Home Page

<www.princeton.edu/~abelson/index.html>

If you are serious about market research, you have to use this site. A terrific help to anyone planning to survey a market. Plus a lot more.

U.S. Business Advisor

<www.business.gov/>

Truthfully labeled "the one-stop electronic link to government."

U.S. Federal Trade Commission

<www.ftc.gov>

Major resource, especially if you plan to grow a consumer-oriented business. Plenty of free information.

Welcome to Hoover's Online!

Good for info on publicly traded companies, IPOs, and so forth. Some
  areas are by subscription only.

Software

NEBS Software

Some of the best software for small businesses is the One-Write Plus®
accounting and payroll software from NEBS. One-Write Plus generates
over 60 reports and financial statements, many of which may be customized by the user. For more information contact NEBS Software, Inc., 20
Industrial Park Drive, Nashua, NH 03062 or call 800-882-5254.

Additional Resources

Small Business Development Centers (SBDCs). Call your state university
or the Small Business Administration (SBA) to find the SBDC nearest you.
Far and away the best free management program available, SBDCs provide
expert assistance and training in every aspect of business management.
Don't ignore this resource.

Service Corps of Retired Executives (SCORE). Sponsored by the Small
Business Administration (SBA), SCORE provides free counseling and also
a series of workshops and seminars for small businesses. Of special interest, SCORE offers a Business Planning Workshop that includes a 30-minute
video produced specifically for SCORE by Upstart Publishing and funded
by Paychex, Inc. There are over 500 SCORE chapters nationwide. For more
information, contact the SBA office nearest you and ask about SCORE.

Small Business Administration (SBA). The SBA offers a number of management assistance programs. If you are assigned a capable Management
Assistance Officer, you have an excellent resource. The SBA is worth a
visit, if only to leaf through their extensive literature.

Padgett Thompson Seminars. Offers business seminars on specific personnel topics for a reasonable fee. Call them at 800-255-4141 for topics and
prices. Their seminar entitled Hiring and Firing is excellent, well-docu-
mented, and useful. Good handout materials are included.

Colleges and Universities. Most have business courses. Some have SBDCs,
others have more specialized programs. Some have small-business expertise—the University of New Hampshire, for example, has two schools that
provide direct small-business management assistance.

Libraries. Do not forget to take advantage of the information readily available at your local library.

GLOSSARY

"acid test" ratio   Cash, plus other assets that can be immediately converted to cash, should equal or exceed current liabilities. The formula used to determine the ratio is as follows:

$$\frac{\text{cash plus receivables (net) plus marketable securities}}{\text{current liabilities}}$$

The "acid test" ratio is one of the most important credit barometers used by lending institutions, as it indicates the abilities of a business enterprise to meet its current obligations.

aging receivables   A scheduling of accounts receivable according to the length of time they have been outstanding. This shows which accounts are not being paid in a timely manner and may reveal any difficulty in collecting long overdue receivables. This may also be an important indicator of developing cash flow problems.

AIDA (attention, interest, desire, action)   Acronym used to remember the sequence of steps in making a sale: gain the prospect's Attention, arouse Interest in the product or service, arouse Desire for the product or service, secure Action (a decision to buy or not to buy).

amortization   To liquidate on an installment basis; the process of gradually paying off a liability over a period of time, (i.e., a mortgage is amortized by periodically paying off part of the face amount of the mortgage).

assets   The valuable resources, or properties and property rights owned by an individual or business enterprise.

balance sheet   An itemized statement that lists the total assets, liabilities, and net worth of a given business to reflect its financial condition at a given moment.

benefits (of a product or service)   The emotional or other end results that your products or services provide. "My factories make cosmetics; we sell hope." Hope is the benefit.

breakeven analysis Mathematical analysis which establishes the sales point at which the business neither makes nor loses money.

breakeven point The volume of sales at which the business neither makes a profit nor suffers a loss.

capital Capital funds are those funds that are needed for the base of the business. Usually they are put into the business in a fairly permanent form such as fixed assets or plant and equipment, or are used in other ways that are not recoverable in the short run unless the entire business is sold.

capital equipment Equipment used to manufacture a product, provide a service, or sell, store, and deliver merchandise. Such equipment will not be sold in the normal course of business but will be used and worn out or be consumed over time as business is conducted.

capitalization The total funds invested in a business, including equity, debt, and retained surplus.

cash flow The actual movement of cash within a business—cash inflow minus cash outflow. A term used to designate the reported net income of a corporation plus amounts charged off for depreciation, depletion, amortization, and extraordinary charges to reserves, which are bookkeeping deductions and not actually paid out in cash. Used to offer a better indication of the ability of a firm to meet its own obligations and to pay dividends, rather than the conventional net income figure.

cash position See **liquidity.**

collateral An asset pledged to a lender in order to support the loan.

commodity A basic or staple item, such as milk, that (in this context) is usually bought on a price basis.

competition Businesses competing for the same market dollars as you; may be direct (selling the same product or service in the same way to the same people) or indirect.

competitive advantage Those aspects of your business which give it an edge over your competition.

competitive analysis Structured look at your competitors to find out how you and they differ (or do not differ).

competitive position How you stack up against your competition.

core markets Those markets you won't give up no matter what you have to do to keep them.

current assets Cash or other items that will normally be turned into cash within one year, and assets that will be used up in the operations of a firm within one year.

current liabilities Amounts owed that will ordinarily be paid by a firm within one year. Such items include accounts payable, wages payable, taxes payable, the current portion of a long-term debt, and interest and dividends payable.

current ratio A ratio of a firm's current assets to its current liabilities. Because a current ratio includes the value of inventories that have not yet been sold, it does not offer the best evaluation of the firm's current status. The "acid test" ratio, covering the most liquid of current assets, produces a better evaluation.

customer base   Customers who are (all things being equal) going to stick with you.

debt   Refers to borrowed funds, whether from your own coffers or from other individuals, banks, or institutions. It is generally secured with a note, which in turn may be secured by a lien against property or other assets. Ordinarily, the note states repayment and interest provisions, which vary greatly in both amount and duration, depending upon the purpose, source, and terms of the loan. Some debt is convertible, that is, it may be changed into direct ownership of a portion of a business under certain stated conditions.

demand   The desire for a commodity together with the ability to pay for it; also, the amount people are ready and able to buy at a certain price. Think "supply and demand."

demographics   (1) The statistical study of human populations, especially with reference to size and density, distribution, and vital statistics.

demographics   (2) Relating to the dynamic balance of a population, especially with regard to density and capacity for expansion or decline.

demographic segmentation   A marketing analysis that targets groups of prospects by factors such as sex, age, marital status, income, occupation, family size, and education (from *Forecasting Sales and Planning Profits,* Kenneth E. Marino).

direct mail   Sale of products directly to the customer through the mail, usually via catalogs, thus cutting out the retail link in the sales chain.

distinctive competence   What you do best, preferably better than anyone else in your market. Wal-Mart's distinctive competence lies in its distribution methods, which enable rapid changes in response to customer demand.

distribution   The delivery or conveyance of a good or service to a market.

distribution channel   The chain of intermediaries linking the producer of a good to the consumer.

equity   Equity is the owner's investment in the business. Unlike capital, equity is what remains after the liabilities of the company are subtracted from the assets—thus it may be greater than or less than the capital invested in the business. Equity investment carries with it a share of ownership and usually a share in profits, as well as some say in how the business is managed.

external analysis   Analysis of those factors outside your business that present opportunities or threats.

facilities brochure   Promotional brochure stating what you do and why you will be able to deliver.

gross profit   Net sales (sales minus returned merchandise, discounts, or other allowances) minus the cost of goods sold.

guaranty   A pledge by a third party to repay a loan in the event that the borrower cannot.

income statement   A statement of income and expenses for a given period of time.

internal analysis   Analysis of the internal strengths and weaknesses of the business.

inventory   The materials owned and held by a business firm, including new materials, intermediate products and parts, work-in-process, and finished goods, intended either for internal consumption or for sale.

liquidity   A term used to describe the solvency of a business, and that has special reference to the degree of readiness in which assets can be converted into cash without a loss. Also called **cash position**. If a firm's current assets cannot be converted into cash to meet current liabilities, the firm is said to be *illiquid.*

loan agreement   A document that states what a business can or cannot do as long as it owes money to (usually) a bank. A loan agreement may place restrictions on the owner's salary, or dividends, the amount of other debt, working capital limits, sales, or the number of additional personnel.

loans   Debt money for private business is usually in the form of bank loans, which, in a sense, are personal because a private business can be harder to evaluate in terms of creditworthiness and degree of risk. A secured loan is a loan that is backed up by a claim against some asset or assets of a business. An unsecured loan is backed by the faith the bank has in the borrower's ability to pay back the money.

long-term liabilities   These are liabilities (expenses) that will not mature within the next year.

logo   Short for logotype.

logotype   Distinctive company signature, trademark, typeface, motto, etc.

market share   Your percentage share of the markets you operate in. A business is usually considered dominant when it captures 25 percent of a market.

marketing orientation   As contrasted with a product orientation, a marketing orientation looks to what the market wants as a way to maintain its focus.

mission statement   Short statement of the raison d'être for the business, what it wants to accomplish and be famous for.

net worth   The owner's equity in a given business represented by the excess of the total assets over the total amounts owed to outside creditors (total liabilities) at a given moment in time. Also, the net worth of an individual as determined by deducting the amount of all personal liabilities from the total value of personal assets. Generally refers to tangible net worth, that is, does not include goodwill, and so forth.

note   The basic business loan, a note represents a loan that will be repaid, or substantially reduced 30, 60, or 90 days later at a stated interest rate.

These are short term, and unless they are made under a line of credit, a separate loan application is needed for each loan and each renewal.

partnership   A legal relationship created by the voluntary association of two or more persons to carry on as co-owners of a business for profit; a type of business organization in which two or more persons agree on the amount of their contributions (capital and effort) and on the distribution of profits, if any.

point of purchase (POP) displays   Displays set up in the store or place of business to entice passers-by to buy.

positioning   A marketing method based on determining what market niche your business should fill and how it should promote its products or services in light of competitive and other forces. "Positioning is what you do to the mind of the prospect. That is, you position the product in the mind of the prospect." (Ries & Trout: *Positioning: The Battle for Your Mind*, p. 2)

price inelasticity   Not sensitive to changes in price (said of demand) product differentiation: establishing differences between one product or service and its competitor.

product positioning   See positioning (above).

pro forma   A projection or an estimate of what may result in the future from actions in the present. A pro forma financial statement is one that shows how the actual operations of a business will turn out if certain assumptions are realized.

profit   The excess of the selling price over all costs and expenses incurred in making a sale. Also, the reward to the entrepreneur for the risks assumed by him or her in the establishment, operations, and management of a given enterprise or undertaking.

promotional pyramid   A visual representation of the steps required to move a prospect from being unaware of your business's existence to actually purchasing your goods and services.

sales forecast   Educated guesstimates of future revenues segmentation: dividing markets into smaller groups that share specific characteristics such as age, education, and income level thought to be decision-making factors in purchasing your product or service.

shopping the competition   Going to the competition's place of business as a customer to see how they serve the public, and what the product or service lines are in hopes of finding weaknesses to exploit.

sole proprietorship or **proprietorship**   A type of business organization in which one individual owns the business. Legally, the owner *is* the business and personal assets are typically exposed to liabilities of the business.

SWOT analysis   SWOT stands for strengths, weaknesses, opportunities, threats. A method of analyzing the business to decide what to stress, what to minimize, and how. Forces a look at both internal and external forces.

subchapter S corporation or **tax option corporation**   A corporation that has elected under Subchapter S of the IRS Tax Code (by unanimous consent of its shareholders) not to pay any corporate tax on its income and, instead, to have the shareholders pay taxes on it, even though it is not distributed. Shareholders of a tax option corporation are also entitled to deduct, on the individual returns, their shares of any net operating loss sustained by the corporation, subject to limitations in the tax code. In many respects, Subchapter S permits a corporation to behave for tax purposes as a proprietorship or partnership.

takeover   The acquisition of one company by another company.

target market   The specific individuals, distinguished by socioeconomic, demographic and/or interest characteristics, who are the most likely potential customers for the goods and/or services of a business.

term loans   Loans that are either secured or unsecured, usually for periods of more than a year to as many as ten. Term loans are paid off like a mortgage: so many dollars per month for so many years. The most common uses of term loans are for equipment and other fixed asset purposes, working capital, and real estate.

unique selling proposition (USP)   An idea from Rosser Reeves, ad giant of the 1950s, who said that it was most important to determine what is special about your product so you can differentiate it from all its competitors.

value and lifestyles study (VALS)   A study that segments the buying public into seven value and lifestyle categories, from early adopters to survivalists.

word-of-mouth advertising   Relying on current satisfied customers to tell their friends and associates about your business. Usually only works in reverse: dissatisfied customers tell 11 to 20 others about how lousy your business is, while satisfied customers keep it to themselves. Used thoughtfully, this can be a powerful medium. Customers can help spread the good news if you make it easy for them.

working capital   The difference between current assets and current liabilities. Contrasted with capital, a permanent use of funds, working capital cycles through your business in a variety of forms: inventories, accounts and notes receivable, and cash and securities.

INDEX